Fashion and Women's Attitudes
in the
Nineteenth Century

The Village Orphan.

From an engraving in the *Lady's Magazine*, for March 1800

Fashion and Women's Attitudes in the Nineteenth Century

C. WILLETT CUNNINGTON

Dover Publications, Inc.
Mineola, New York

Bibliographical Note

This Dover edition, first published in 2003, is an unabridged republication of the work originally published in 1936 by The Macmillan Company, New York, under the title *Feminine Attitudes in the Nineteenth Century.*

Library of Congress Cataloging-in-Publication Data

Cunnington, C. Willett (Cecil Willett), 1878–1961.
 [Feminine attitudes in the nineteenth century]
 Fashion and women's attitudes in the nineteenth century / C. Willett Cunnington.
      p. cm.
 Originally published: Feminine attitudes in the nineteenth century. London : W. Heinemann, 1935.
   ISBN 0-486-43190-8 (pbk.)
   1. Women—Great Britain—Attitudes. 2. Women—Great Britain—History—19th century. 3. England—Social life and customs—19th century. I. Title.

HQ1593.C8 2003
305.4'0941—dc21

2003055325

Manufactured in the United States by Courier Corporation
43190804
www.doverpublications.com

PREFACE

To C. B. Mortlock:

In the good old days of Victorian melodrama it was customary for the Betrayed to lay her offspring on the Villain's doorstep, and then rush blindly into the snowstorm. As you, morally at least, are responsible for this book, it is fitting that your name should stand here in a white sheet. . . . For me, the snowstorm. . . .

It was you who led me into committing one of the most indiscreet forms of writing, the explanatory. As a nation we dislike being explained, and it is specially dangerous to explain the Feminine mind; there is always the risk of being understood. However, the Nineteenth Century cannot now defend itself, and the Victorians are considered fair game. Their merits are apt to be overlooked, and I have therefore tried to indicate some of those gifts with which the average woman was adorned, making it the great Feminine Century in History. It is high time that someone threw at her a bouquet or two. Here is mine.

You, as a critic, may cavil at the extended meaning I have given to the weather-beaten word "Gothic." You will remember that Gothic Art has been defined by an eminent authority, as "the

v

Art of constructing buttressed buildings." How, you ask, can a word so limited to architecture be applied to the elusive qualities of the feminine mind and body? I have used it to denote more than an Art: an Attitude, of which the Art is but an outward expression.

We need a word embracing both the Romantic and the Sentimental postures by which our race is notably distinguished from others; the gift of being able to distort or conceal facts to suit our feelings. The former is essentially the Romantic and the latter the Sentimental Attitude. Thanks to it the Englishman of last century was able to adjust Truth to suit his needs, while the Englishwoman, still more richly endowed, was able to impose herself upon him. She studied to create a peculiar illusion about herself, her mind and body, and her skill deserves our admiration. We have only to read the great masculine novelists of that era to perceive how successfully she concealed her real self from them.

Yet had she not "organs, dimensions, senses, affections, passions" and so forth? How ingeniously her human qualities were buttressed by romantic ideals helping to sustain the great illusion! How carefully the fundamentals, on which her charms were based, were hidden! Surely it is now permissible to remove some of the scaffolding? It was the Gothic instinct which built up that elaborate decoration round the mind, and in the same spirit concealed the body.

Preface

Indeed, as we view the Victorian Lady in the full canoply of Gothic masquerade we perceive in a fresh light the accuracy of that definition: "the art of constructing buttressed buildings." Somewhere within that monolith was hidden a creature of flesh and blood. What did she think of it all? Was she conscious of the pose, with instincts chuckling, or was she playing the game blindfold?

Exploring the ruins of that Gothic epoch we find enough to show that the Victorian woman was the supreme expression of its genius. We unearth, alas! a mind tantalising in its reticence. What, for instance, was her real opinion of the Victorian Man? Were her movements governed by chance or calculation? Is the modern Woman the conscious product of a century's manœuvring or merely an unforeseen result? There are, unhappily, not enough fragments discoverable to decide such points.

You must not, therefore, expect to have exposed to your critical eye more of the Victorian Lady than a legless torso. Besides, "there is a decency to be observit," and I shrink from exhuming the bones of my grandmothers except in a spirit of admiring reverence.

CONTENTS

ILLUSTRATIONS

xi

CHAPTER I

Introduction

THE aim of this book is to describe the series of Attitudes which were assumed by Englishwomen during the 19th century: that is to say, those unconscious postures of mind and body which members of a social group will display as features in common.

The explanation of these Attitudes is obtained by inferences drawn from contemporary evidence, and wherever possible from feminine sources. Such a history of conventional Attitudes is necessarily concerned with types and not with individuals, so that for this purpose Eminent Victorians are of less importance than those multitudes of mute inglorious females of whom no biography has ever been written, who never did or said or thought anything that distinguished them from the mass of women of their day, and who have left as their only memorial—the present generation.

The typical Woman of any period is a creature

1

governed by Fashions, Customs, Habits and Instincts.

Fashion may be defined as a taste shared by a large number of people for a short space of time. (A taste shared by only a few is not a fashion, but a peculiarity.) A taste persisting long enough ceases to be a Fashion, and becomes a Custom. A Custom which endures still longer becomes a Habit, and a Habit of immeasureable antiquity becomes established as an Instinct. So that an Instinct is simply a Fashion which has been found so convenient that it has never been given up.

Fashions change rapidly; Customs slowly; Habits seldom, and Instincts never. Where women are concerned, "Fashion," in the popular sense, refers to personal adornments, but it should include all the temporary tastes and doings which she shares with the rest of her social group. It is a Fashion to wear—let us say —a crinoline, or to smoke cigarettes, but the wearing of a skirt is a Custom, while the wearing of clothing at all is a Habit, and the desire to attract the other sex is an Instinct.

In addition to sex-attraction the feminine Attitude is greatly influenced by the Herd Instinct, or the wish to imitate, in appearance and conduct, those in the same social group. Both of these Instincts are much stronger in Women than in Men; in primitive states of society the male could obtain satisfaction by force without troubling to attract, and could ignore the Herd by reason of his greater physical strength which permitted him to roam away from it if he chose. The female, however, had to look to the Herd for physical and sexual protection, and she has consequently always retained an instinctive desire to win the benevolent approval of it. For her own sake she has cultivated an extremely sensitive "Herd Instinct," which prompts her to approve of orthodox and disapprove of unorthodox conduct.

To be "in the fashion" gives her a peculiar glow of sensuous satisfaction; indeed, a woman of fashion has said that the consciousness of being well-dressed imparts a peace of mind greater than is obtained from any religion.

It is the instinct of the Herd to dislike originality, and it ensures its healthy persistence by rigorous disapproval of abnormal manifestations of the sex instinct.

As society has developed women have striven to increase their powers of sex-attraction, and Man has gradually been compelled to woo instead of taking by force. In order to add to its fascination women have restricted the expression of the instinct within well-defined limits, by means of a host of Taboos.

Concealment of the sexual features of the body was an early device, and clothing was invented to add to the mystery; gradually the practice extended to the concealment (or affected concealment, for the symbolism is the same) of non-sexual regions, so that occasional exposure of them would attract the attention of the other sex. Hence the gloved hand, which the Victorian fine lady would maintain even indoors.

Uncovering such regions would eventually come to be considered a delicate compliment, as when a man takes off his hat to a lady. In his subconscious mind is the barbarous thought that he would gladly take off everything for her sake.

A further stage of refined implication is a reluctance to use words reminiscent of the unclothed state; euphemisms are employed for "naked," "breast," "leg," "stomach." The Victorian period was peculiarly rich in such by-play, when, for instance, it was indelicate to offer a lady the *leg* of a chicken; by association of ideas the mention of underclothing is tabooed, and the nice-minded speak vaguely of "lingerie." The

4

Victorian matron, driven by unavoidable facts, resorted to an interesting condition, and little strangers were discovered under gooseberry bushes . . . until at last the Perfect Lady became a human being only by inference.

The origin of these social Taboos is readily forgotten; from being in some measure useful they have merged into the vague domain of "good manners." That they are now wholly irrational is shown by the strange variations which are permitted; conduct or costume "decent" in one locality is "indecent" in another, and even different hours of the day have different rules of decency, and these arbitrary rules change from year to year. Their only function is to sustain an interest in sex-attraction devices. Most women instinctively feel that absolute nudity, for example, tends to diminish sex-attraction; hence their shrinking from it, while a pretence in that direction is alluring. To arouse curiosity but not to satisfy it too readily is Woman's aim. The cult of Modesty, which in primitive conditions had been a protection, becomes, as civilisation advances, a tactical manœuvre, camouflaged as a Virtue, which is discarded whenever inconvenient or no longer necessary.

The 19th century woman, whose economic

position was still largely dependent on her powers of sex-attraction, made a virtue of necessity, and in her hands modesty became a fine art.

The normal woman's psychology possesses the elements of both Sentimentalism and Exhibitionism. The former is an over-charge of feeling so that events, especially those concerned with her sex-life, are viewed through an emotional fog whereby their shapes are agreeably distorted; reality tends to dissolve into fantasy. The Sentimentalist tries to attract the Man by sustained illusions; she swathes her mind in emotions and her body in clothing.

The Exhibitionist, on the other hand, has an instinctive desire to expose herself, body and mind, so as to *compel* Man's attention by a short cut, and merely to be noticed by him affords her pleasure.

Obviously the two Attitudes of mind are essentially antagonistic, and in the normal woman, under normal conditions, balance each other; she is capable of using either as occasion demands.

But abnormal social conditions can tip the balance and produce an exaggeration of the one, and a diminution of the other, throughout a community. When a Nation, or even a section of it, has been subjected to an intense emotional strain, the emotional capacity is exhausted, and a generation grows up with, for the time being, a reduced power of feeling—in a word, Unsentimental. Such a generation invariably displays marked signs of Exhibitionism.

On the other hand, when a Nation, or a section of it, experiences a period of comfortable prosperity and freedom from anxiety, it tends to exude with well-fed Sentimentality, especially if, like the English, it is by Nature richly endowed with that quality already.

The opulent Victorians suffered from a wealth of feeling which overflowed in every direction.

Sentimentalism and Exhibitionism each gives rise to different methods of sex-attraction; the former leans to the romantic, the crude instinct being concealed under a glamour, and in extreme cases is apt to be distorted into Masochism and Sadism. Exhibitionism, on the other hand, inclines to realistic forms of expression; the crude instinct is admired, and in extreme cases leads to the abnormality, Perversion.

Each type of mind tends, of course, to rationalise its impulse; the Sentimentalist affects a worship of propriety and reticence, while the Exhibitionist cultivates sunbathing and sex

7

chatter. The latter views the Sentimentalist with contempt, who turns from the Exhibitionist in horror. The 19th century supplied excellent examples of each phase. Being an extremely sentimental race by nature, our normal attitude of mind is Sentimentalism, which for centuries has governed our tastes, our modes of artistic expression, and our manners of sex-attraction. It is natural for us to shun realism and to be shocked by the "naked truth."

In Art we have an age-old predilection towards the Gothic, which is essentially a method of drawing a veil over the harsher aspects of Truth. But when Sentimentalism has undergone a temporary eclipse as the result of adverse circumstances, we turn, for the time being, towards its antithesis. The "Classical" form of Art is then admired for its frank statement of Truth. Its unemotional uprightness of line seems to afford repose for our exhausted feelings. Such occasions in our history have been few; they have generally followed some great social strain, for example, the Great War, the Napoleonic War, and, in the 14th century, the Black Death (when Gothic architecture abruptly changed into what is called the Perpendicular style). At such times we become impatient of decorative illusions, and demand the simple, the stark, the real . . . which naturally find expression in current modes of Art, Thought and Conduct. Such was the spirit prevailing during the first twenty years of the 19th century, the "Vertical Epoch."

With a return to more normal conditions and a Gothic frame of mind, from 1821 onwards the Nation recovered its habitual relish for disguising reality by refinements; that is to say, by concealments, evasions and distortions of naked truth.

We shall see how this Gothic Epoch began with a Romantic Attitude of mind and body, followed by an ultra-sentimental, in which the domestic virtues were idealised, these phases occupying the period 1821–1865. As we should expect, during this period Art was markedly Gothic in style.

The last third of the century, from 1865 onwards, was occupied, psychologically, by attempted adjustments of the sex relationship, and covert hostility. It was a period when the vision of an alternative career began to show above the Englishwoman's horizon, with all its possibilities, doubts and dangers, so that she was torn between its attractions and the safe servitude of sex. Her attitude was therefore one of hesitation and indecision. It will be seen how discords in the fashions of her dress betrayed this mental conflict; the period might be described as "Debased Gothic," with Curves as its principal feature.

All through the century the significance of Fashions in dress has to be emphasised, because for the most part it was Woman's chief or only means of self-expression.

It is therefore necessary to meet a possible criticism at this point. If the Englishwoman's fashions in dress are unconscious reflections of her mental attitude, how will such a line of argument explain similar changes of Fashion in other Nations remote from ourselves, and exposed to conditions entirely different, or even in a near country such as France, whose people are notoriously less sentimental than the English? How is it that with such different racial temperaments their Fashions should have been identical? Besides, have we not almost invariably accepted women's fashions ready made, as it were, from France? In a word, are not women's fashions simply the work of designing conspirators secreted somewhere on the Continent?

To take the last point first: the prevailing style of Dress is always associated with a similar style in other Arts. In the Vertical Epoch the vertical emphasis was in marked evidence in Arts entirely beyond the influence of the dress designer. The extreme form of Gothic dress occurred in the 40's and 50's, at the height of the "Victorian Gothic" movement. Pugin did not, surely, derive his inspiration from the fashionable dressmakers? Moreover, if we trace the very beginnings of such artistic movements, we discover that actually the Fashion in Dress lags slightly behind that in other Arts, and tends to linger on after they have changed. It is clear, then, that some widespread and profound influence comes over a Nation—or at least its more sensitive sections—affecting all its forms of artistic expression, of which Dress is but one. The fashion-designer, in fact, does not create the popular demand; he merely satisfies it.

Nor is the influence of the individual (whether a Great Personage or even a Cinema star) more than trifling; such people may affect details, the precise tilt of the hat, the exact site for a smudge of paint, but they cannot make a whole Nation adopt a particular taste in Art and maintain it for a generation. It is inherently much more probable that the Individual, no matter how eminent, is herself unconsciously inspired by the spirit of her day. From her position she may be one of the first to display the new fashion and to be noticed; but even then she has not created the impulse.

Moreover we are apt to overlook the enormous number of instances where the taste of the Great Person has failed to impress itself on the fashions of her time because that taste was not in harmony with the inclinations of the community. For example, Queen Victoria occupied the most prominent position possible, with a host of marked habits, tastes and characteristics, all perfectly familiar to the Nation; nevertheless in no instance did she affect the fashions of her time; indeed, during the last two-thirds of her reign she viewed the steady advance of Woman's Emancipation and sex-readjustment with cold hostility. Her opinion was well known. Yet it was ignored. In fact, whenever she consciously applied her enormous influence on Fashion, it completely failed.*

On the other hand when the morbid Sentimentalism of the period developed into a passion for masochistic display, it chimed in so happily with her own nature that she made widowhood

---

*It is strange but true that neither the Queen nor any of her daughters have ever originated a fashion, or set the mode as to style . . . However, it is certain that the Royal Family have had no influence of any kind on the dress of the age, and have added nothing to the annals of historic costume.—From *The Burlington Magazine*, Vol. II.   May to August, 1881.

and its gloomy trappings almost a symbol of the Nation's attitude.

During the century the various Great Ladies and Notorious Beauties left no mark on the Fashions except, perhaps, a stray ornament—a Langtry bonnet, a Nightingale cloak. We might equally assume that the Gladstone bag was directly inspired by the creative genius of that eminent person, or that Wellington designed his boots.

That unimportant little social group calling themselves the "Smart Set," are mainly agents, conscious or otherwise, of the Trade, and the modes sported by them for a day are not Fashions, but Advertisements.

The influence of common sense has never checked a Fashion in its flood; artists have shuddered in vain, doctors have prophesied disease, theologians have thundered out damnation; even the Press fails. . . . Woman, triumphant, moves from mood to mood, expressing each in the way she does because she must. We can recognise, now, that the Fashions of the 19th century were far from being mere accidents, but were, each in their way, singularly appropriate to the attitude of mind expected of a woman by the man of her world. By her appearance, manner and mode of life, she expressed his ideal: romantic or doll-like or dignified, as the case might be. To meet his exacting requirements she could alter the texture of her mind, and even the shape of her body. In our own post-war years, for example, when, owing to economic difficulties, the young man of that day, shrinking from the idea of marriage and a family, preferred the un-maternal type of girl, immediately there was produced a supply amounting to a glut; hair was cropped schoolboy fashion, breasts were obliterated by compressors, slimming practised to remove the last traces of feminine curves—a process demanding extraordinary self-denial—and masculine clothing and habits borrowed in the effort to obliterate the "Eternal Feminine."

When, on the other hand, times are prosperous and Man is attracted to the sentimental-maternal type, Woman strives to indicate that she is fitted for the rôle; she emphasises the physical distinctions of her sex; draws attention to the curves of her figure which are then sex-attractive; and the Fashion of her dress is designed to emphasise them.

When we consider the extraordinary discomforts that at different epochs Woman has tolerated—breathless constriction, high heels, trailing skirts, the burden of too many, and the misery of too few clothes, to say nothing of the disfigurements of paints, stains, deformities and mutilations, it would be a poor compliment to her intelligence to assume that a woman follows fashion except by the force of a compelling instinct.

It is a curious error to suppose that Englishwomen accept their fashions in dress from France. They do, no doubt, accept—and very gratefully—the French technical skill in expressing Fashions, but careful study of the Fashions of both countries during the 19th century shows that they only succeed in crossing the Channel when they happen to be good illustrations of our mental attitude; actually Fashions are seldom identical in the two countries, but it happened that two such close neighbours were frequently subjected to simultaneous emotional stresses—the Napoleonic wars, the Romantic revival of the 20's, the middle-class revolt of the 30's, the upper-class prosperity of the 50's and 60's, and its decline in the 80's, and the psychology of both Nations being affected in similar ways, we should expect similar Fashions to result.

It cannot be disputed that Women's Fashions are no longer confined to the country of their origin, but tend to spread over the world; they start, however, in the Nation whose culture dominates others. It may be added that in the 19th century there was no such domination by France over England, who was perfectly satisfied with her cultural superiority, and had no inclination to borrow, but rather to lend.

The causes of English Fashions in the 19th century must be sought for, not abroad, but at home; they were inspired "by the sublime instincts of an ancient People."

During most of that century Woman was moulded by rigid customs and habits, which helped materially to produce her Attitudes. The Etiquette Books reveal how precise were the regulations of deportment to indicate the finer shades of rank, the nice distinctions between the Matron and the Maiden, the subtleties you must observe: things that revealed whether you were indeed the Perfect Lady or only "not quite." The verdict might turn on a hair—the management of a teacup—the inflection of a "how d'you do?" In the Victorian period especially, an enormous portion of "good manners" became merely tests of social position, symbols of good breeding.

The feminine mind has always preferred the symbolic to a more direct mode of expression, and in the Victorian era it rose to the dignity of a ritual. Consider, for example, the changes of appearance that were thought to be necessary by the Perfect Lady; among the Best People the dressing-room was a factory of Beauty, where the lady's maid was overseer; there the lady of leisure toiled; before she appeared in public she had assumed a Peignoir; about the house she must wear a "morning dress"; for shopping a slightly more elegant one was required to indicate to the shopman the exact degree of exorbitance she was prepared to tolerate. Of an afternoon, the Visiting Costume called for extraordinary selection, according to the rank of those about to be visited. On occasions of special moment further elaboration was needed, for Garden Parties, Flower Shows, and attendance at Public Places, while something more thoughtful would suit the atmosphere of a Picture Gallery.

Later, the Dinner Gown, "quiet" or "full," as the case might be, or, on occasions, an elaborate Confection for the Opera . . . and as the climax of all earthly ambitions, there would be the COURT DRESS. There were, of course, other critical, if less sublime, moments in her life, each demanding distinctive costumes. Once, at least, she was destined to wear a Wedding Dress; up till the 40's this was usually similar to an evening dress, with low neck and short sleeves; later, it was in the style of an afternoon dress, glorified with orange-blossom, veil and white satin prayer-book. The colour was generally, but by no means invariably, cream or white; pale lavender was a popular alternative.

At frequent intervals in her social life she would find herself suddenly plunged into "mourning," the precise shades and duration of which were an anxious study. In such case it was safer to rely, not upon one's feelings, but upon some guide-book, which would infallibly distinguish between the sorrow one ought to feel for a deceased Aunt or for a mere Cousin. There was a defined shade and period for each particular degree of relationship, so that she could express in unmistakable form the exact intensity of her grief. Moreover, it was her duty to suffer as long for her husband's relations as for her own; one reads of a Victorian lady complaining with some bitterness, that although married seven years she had not yet been able to wear her trousseau dresses, on account of her relations-in-law who had died off during that period. Had they departed *en masse* she could have borne it, but their thoughtless going off at intervals had entailed continuous mourning for seven years, at the end of which her trousseau was, of course, hopelessly unfashionable.

All through the century mourning was elaborate. A special uniform was reserved for the widow, of black crepe, worn for a year and a day, when she "slighted her mourning" and went into black, which it was good taste to wear for the rest of her days. A notable figure, the Victorian widow, with dress, veil, gloves, muff, parasol and shoes all black, and handkerchief and visiting cards deeply edged, so that she seemed as one in disgrace. It appeared that the punishment for losing a husband was worse than the crime.

In the use of colours in women's dress another form of symbolism may appear; an intense colour used, unconsciously, to draw attention to a particular region, or as a device of Prudery, to draw away attention from some vital part. The general colour sense of the century, as shown in Women's dress, revealed a taste for Harmony during the first two-thirds, and for strong Contrasts during the last third of it. It would be a rash assumption to speak of any period as one of "bad taste"; taste is ephemeral, and in any case the historian's personal opinion is irrelevant; but we can, with some show of reason, argue that a preference for harmony in colour suggests an harmonious mental attitude, and that the growing sense of dissatisfaction evidenced by women during the last third of the century was responsible for the harshness of their taste in colour. They were no longer in harmony with their mental environment, and they symbolised a mental conflict by discordant colours in dress. If, then, a widespread taste for disharmony in Art is evidence of a widespread dissatisfaction with things as they are, to dismiss such epochs as "degenerate" would be to misinterpret what is, in reality, a symptom of progress. We ought rather to regard the periods of "bad Art" in our history with a certain feeling of gratitude.

Symbolism is an unconscious way of expressing hidden thoughts, and is most used, of course, when conventions forbid more outspoken methods; there were periods, as in the 80's, when its use was peculiarly significant, but all through the Victorian era, symbols were abundantly employed by women.

The small hand, and therefore the tight glove, indicated that the owner was above having to do manual work; the huge crinoline signified that the wearer occupied a large space in the social world; the trailing skirt that she did not belong to the "walking classes," and the stiff corset proved that she was a woman of unbending rectitude.

May we not also read in the small waist a mute appeal for the support of the masculine arm?

Jewelry readily lent itself to subtle implications; articles which embrace the wearer, such as the necklace and bracelet, have an obvious symbolism, while the Victorian idea of modesty was emphasised by elaborate concealment, in which symbols of the forbidden subject kept peeping out unawares; a costume burlesquing the sexual curves; elaborate pains taken to conceal the breasts, with still more elaborate pains to draw attention to them; sometimes the suppressed thought would reveal itself in patterns on the dress outlining the terra incognita, a conspicuous fencing-off of no-man's-land. Yet the instinct would attempt a break-through. . . .

A sublime specimen of an evening dress of the 90's (now in the Victoria and Albert Museum), is almost indelicately décolletée, with the gap filled in with velvet of a *flesh colour*, to create the illusion of nudity. The spirit is willing but the flesh is weak.

A study of the symbolism in Women's Fashions affords a valuable insight into their minds. The rich fields of the 19th century need further exploration, but even a cursory survey suggests that the Victorian lady, in the chambers of her mind, was far from resembling the heroine of the Victorian novel. Of course, the true meaning of symbolic acts, being the outcome of subconscious impulses, is never admitted or even recognised by the user. By a process of "rationalisation" ingenious explanations will be put forward; nudity will be justified as hygienic, and excess of clothing by a fear of chill; sinuous lines are but graceful, and things shown aren't meant to be looked at; display is frankness, and concealment purity of mind.

The average Englishwoman of the 19th century has not received the credit that is her due, and the significance of her Attitudes has not been sufficiently appreciated. They were moves in a great game, at which she was, on the whole, supremely successful, especially when she was content to use the faculties with which Nature had endowed her for the purpose with which she was endowed. The ever-changing Attitude of 19th century women reveals other secrets besides their own. As we peer into the depths of their psychology, we catch perpetual reflections of the other sex, and we recognise, with Mrs. Poyser, that "God Almighty made them to match the men."

Chapter II

The Vertical Epoch

B Y 1800 the flood of ideas which the French
Revolution had brought to the surface had
overflowed into this country, where they provoked
intense alarm and disapproval. But mere disapproval of new ideas will not prevent their
germinating, especially if they should fall upon
virgin soil. The mind of the average Englishwoman had been uncultivated and extremely
narrow, but perhaps was not as prejudiced as that
of the average Englishman.

It was the sort of ground on which new ideas,
if they could reach it, might well grow. Probably
they would not have travelled to her if the
Revolution had not been succeeded by a prolonged war affecting the economics of every English home. During most of this epoch England
was engaged in a dreary, expensive contest, too
remote to interest, too tedious to excite the
imagination of the Englishwoman in her home.
One observes that in Jane Austen's novels of this

period the women never mention it; in the contemporary magazines for ladies there are no emotional comments on the sufferings, mental and physical, produced by the war on the home-life of the women. They accepted it as they would have accepted a succession of bad harvests producing a rise in the cost of living, as a misfortune "sent by Providence to try us."

All they were conscious of at the time was the enormous disturbance in the value of things. Change was in the air; certainties became uncertainties; there was a growing sense of unrest.

Whenever an abrupt re-valuation of things occurs on a large scale, there is, inevitably, a re-valuation of ideas. The rising generation of women began—almost—to think, or, at least, to doubt. The structure of Society, the authority of Religion, Woman's position—were these permanently fixed? Was she inevitably, and by the laws of God and Man destined for ever to be subordinate? Permitted to exercise (within strict limits) her feelings but not her intellect; to employ her physical gifts to attract a mate, and her physical functions to produce his offspring; to concentrate her life on small immediate things, and to accept without resistance the domination of Father, Husband and perhaps Son?

24

We can detect, early in the century, faint doubts arising. . . . And the influence of that everlasting war must have been imperceptibly affecting her general outlook.

It must not be forgotten that by 1800 we had already experienced eight years of war, in which we had been, on the whole, persistently unsuccessful, with occasional disgraceful disasters; the five years immediately preceding 1800 were "England's darkest years," leaving the Nation with a sense of defeat and gloom. To the average woman it may not have been a period of emotional anguish so much as one of unbroken depression, which, in the long run, will produce an even more deadening effect on the feelings. We can therefore understand why the ordinary woman in the early years of the new century was said to be "unfeeling" and "unbelieving."

Wars are apt to begin with credulity and end in scepticism; illusions are destroyed and a craving for freedom arises. Restrictions are thrown aside, as a maddened herd will break through its fences. . . . It is a moment when novelty is extraordinarily attractive, and speculative thought is popular currency. In France the woman of fashion, clothed in Ideas— and very little else, loved to recline on classical

25

couches and prattle philosophy; a costume of transparent muslin served to reveal her intellect. It seems a custom, at such disturbing times, for men to discard their religion, and women their underclothing. Eventually, of course, the mood passes and corset and creed resume their sway as aids to an upright life.

Something of this found an echo in England as the new century opened, but there was this essential difference between the two countries; the last eight years had been for the Englishwoman gloomy but dull; the Frenchwoman had experienced ten years of frightful emotional excitement, beginning with an extraordinary outburst of sentimentalism, which had degenerated into an orgy of sadism. By a natural swing of the pendulum she turned towards Exhibitionism with a sense of relief, and indulged in it to an extent which the Englishwoman had not the same inducement to copy. In her manners, her costume, her frame of mind, the Englishwoman's Exhibitionism was never so intense. However, it was sufficient to produce, for the time being, a definite change in the normal character, especially in the rising generation, always the group to which we turn when we want to examine the effects of recent experience.

What, then, was the typical English girl like in the first twenty years of the 19th century? How shall we ascertain her views of life, her reactions, her impulses? How, in a word, can we, with reasonable accuracy, reconstruct her psychology?

We can, of course, get a sort of picture of her from contemporary novelists, but such evidence is wholly objective, and necessarily distorted by the novelist's own outlook; we must also allow for the conventions which a writer has to obey. We want to get at the aspects which, in novels, are discreetly ignored.

We can, however, reconstruct, to some extent, the subjective attitude, by indirect means.

As a guide to the character of a social group, a knowledge of the prevailing *tastes* is better than knowledge of the prevailing *conduct*. Conduct, in civilised communities, is so much controlled by conscious thought, but tastes reveal the natural inclination of the mind.

At the beginning of the 19th century there was a growing number of magazines written especially for women. They provided an important part of the reading matter of the middle and upper class young woman. That they were popular is evidenced by their continuance, in many cases, for a long period of time.

The Ladies' Magazine, or Entertaining Companion for the Fair Sex, Appropriated Solely to their Use and Amusement, ran from 1769 till 1840; *The Ladies' Monthly Museum, or Polite Repository of Amusement and Instruction, being an assemblage of whatever can tend to please the Fancy, interest the Mind, or exalt the Character of the British Fair*, started in 1798 and survived some thirty years. We also find *La Belle Assemblée, addressed particularly to the Ladies*, from 1806 until well into the 60's.

Being popular with their readers, it is fair to assume they exactly suited their tastes; an analysis of such publications, then, will reveal the tastes of the particular social group reading them. In this way we can get an indirect but subjective reconstruction of their mentality.

These magazines contain fiction, articles on current affairs, science, philosophy and literature, as well as a monthly report of news of the day. One observes in this summary accounts of "shocking events," given with a frankness unusual even in the most modern Woman's Journal. In 1804 a trial is reported in which "two men (one being in holy orders)" were charged with having abducted and ravished one Rachael Lee, "to the great displeasure of Almighty God, to the disparagement of the said Rachael, to the discomfiture of her friends, to the evil example of others, against the form of the statute, against the King's peace, His crown and Dignity." It adds that under cross-examination Rachael admitted that when forced into the chaise "she found further resistance useless, and tearing from her breast a camphire bag, she exclaimed—'The charm that has hitherto preserved my virtue is dissolved!' adding as she threw it away—'Now welcome pleasure!'" At this the learned judge observed that the admission was fatal to the prosecution, and the prisoners were accordingly discharged amid loud huzzas from the crowd. . . . This, in a magazine for young ladies, suggests that they were not particularly squeamish about knowing the "facts of life."

The short stories are illuminating. True, they have a moral, but it is ethical rather than religious; tales illustrating abstract virtues, classical rather than Christian. Religion, in fact, is treated as a mode of manners rather than of feelings. The love story has a coolness about it as an episode in Natural History. There is no allusion to the charms of the nursery. There is hardly a reference to outdoor amusements; scenery and the wilder aspects of Nature make no appeal. The events of the interminable war are recorded without pathos or heroics; its emotional appeal as a "good story" is singularly missed. The readers clearly did not want it. The exaggerated sentimentality shown by the Victorians is wholly absent; we find, in 1807, a girl remarking "Sentiment is now considered completely Gothic and canaillish." Indeed, the expression "Gothic" is used as a term of contempt. The sentimental young woman is held up to ridicule, as one perceives in *Sense and Sensibility*. At that time, of course, the word "sensibility" meant our word "sensitiveness," and was a subject for ironical satire.

We get the impression that the average reader for whom these magazines were designed was interested in Ideas rather than in feelings; sceptical rather than romantic; bored by the beauties of Nature, but intrigued by the facts of human nature; without much humour but with a taste for wit. She seems, in a word, to have been a cool, curious and informed young woman, with enthusiasms but no passions. Such is the product of War and Revolution.

Her nature is often revealed in her letters. The following, dated 1807, and obtained from a private source, suggests a very typical girl of her period. It was written from the country to her cousin to whom she later became engaged and married:

My dear William,

I safely received your letter and was happy to hear you had enjoyed yourself so much. I had almost made up my mind not to write as you delayed writing me so long and thought you had nearly forgotten me, or cared but little whether you heard of me or not, and from the formality of your letter I am nearly convinced my opinion was right. I would have you remember that formality in letter writing only proceeds from an indifference towards the person you address. It does not denote that warm friendship you showed me before you left. . . . On Sunday we had a West Country beau come to see us; he took tea here and made fine fun for us (Papa rode out before tea). One of his speeches was—"My Mother had zeven zons runnen, he! he! he!" And when we were going to Meeting he told Ann if he had not zoo vur too goo whoom he would go with us; we thought it was very lucky he had zoo vur too goo. . . . Thursday last week there was a little pudding sent for Ann with Master Jos' compliments. Ann goes a-fishing with him almost every evening; she went last night which was very lucky for me as I wrote part of this while she was gone and got up early this morning to finish it. I have had five thousand interruptions and obliged to run at every footstep . . .

There is no emotional appeal here, but one perceives a quiet deadliness of purpose.

The magazines occasionally contain Letters from Correspondents, which supply further insight into the mind of the Modern Young Woman of those times.

A young lady defends herself from an unjust charge of want of decorum thus: "I am a clergyman's daughter, brought up in a very recluse manner which does not in the least suit my disposition as I always liked a nice game of romps or some such lively amusement. The great imprudence of which I am accused is too much familiarity with a married man; only because I used to play with him and would amuse myself for a whole evening together in combing his hair. This gave umbrage to his wife who very saucily told me it was imprudent to do so, especially before the servants. I saw she was jealous and therefore was determined to plague her so I quarrelled with her and encouraged him to follow me

everywhere which I knew would tease her hand-
somely. . . . Pray tell me what harm can anyone say of me? Am I to blame? What crime
could there be in teasing such a creature? Don't
you think such fools should all meet with a girl
of my turn? With hopes of meeting with your
approbation, I remain, Madam, Yours sincerely . . ."

A somewhat different type of young woman
writes a "war-girl" letter in 1800: "I am a very
pretty girl and not above sixteen. I am universally admired, nay—followed, and even made a
fuss with, and yet, would you believe it!—I have
not a lover in my train! My patience being at
last exhausted I ventured to ask a smart fellow,
one night at Ranelagh, on his comparing me to an
angel, what he meant? 'Upon my soul, Madam,'
he said, looking archly in my face, 'I mean
nothing at all, but one must say something, you
know.' 'You do not think me handsome, then?'
replied I. 'Not think you handsome? Indeed,
but I do! And most sincerely.' 'Yet neither
you nor any man,' replied I, 'attempt to make
serious proposals to me, while you flirt with half
the married women in the town.' Looking full
at me, he burst into a loud laugh. 'Married
women, child, are the only women in the world

to flirt with; for who, in his sober senses, would chuse, in these ticklish and expensive times to have a wife of his own?' You cannot conceive how much I was mortified by this answer. Government ought, surely, to put a stop, by some speedy methods, to the proceedings of the married women in this licentious age who engross the men to themselves, and hinder us poor girls from getting husbands."

The older generation, needless to say, viewed the Modern Young Woman in that epoch with considerable alarm. The magazines abound with comments from shocked old ladies and snorting old gentlemen, bewailing modern tendencies, the total lack of respect, the boldness of behaviour of the girl of to-day, and in particular the extreme indelicacy of her clothing.

In 1806 we read:—"Many young women seem to study how to be disagreeable; if with their own sex they are listless, yawning and discontented; if with the other, the impudent leer, the pert retort, the silly double entendre sicken those who wish to be rational."

As late as 1819 the complaint is echoed:— "That undoubted boldness and spirit of ridicule, that inattention to the aged and self-sufficiency now so general."

The Vertical Epoch

An old lady in 1800 describes her visit to London to see her granddaughters:—"I arrived at half-past six in Portman Square, where I found several coaches and chairs at the door. I walked up to my own apartment and then begged to see my granddaughters; but before I had finished my request in rushed three young ladies that I had not seen since they were children. After the first compliments were over I entreated them to go and finish their dress as I knew the company was arrived; and in the simplicity of my heart I added: 'for you will catch cold, my dear girls, by your attention to your poor grandmother,' for I plainly discovered they had but one petticoat on and I imagined they were in their powdering gowns. This blunder was explained by a loud laugh from the youngest, whilst her Ladyship, in a suppressed tone, told me they were full dressed for the Opera. It was a cold, bleak evening in March, and being old and chilly myself, I absolutely shuddered when I looked at them. . . . The next morning I saw but little of them, but that little I found detrimental to my health, as during their stay in my room they kept me in continual exercise; for, to my great surprise I was told it was no longer the fashion to wear pockets as it spoilt the symmetry of the shape, so that I had to produce from mine scissors, thimble, etc., and I had their silks, thread and paper to pick up myself, for these fine ladies never allow themselves the least exertion. . . . I found they had never been taught to converse except in the common jargon of bon-ton talk. What can such mothers produce but a race of indolent, insignificant beings!"

(But, in point of fact, they produced—the Victorians.)

A description of manners at a fashionable watering-place in 1813, is also instructive:—"I am struck with the want of that reserve and decorum which used formerly to prevail in all promiscuous meetings. As to dress, no distinction exists between mistress and maid, except that one wears a cap. Another wonderful change in the manner of modern days is the multiplication of noise. Nobody now cares how far he disturbs another. Instead of the slow, quiet walk, young ladies now run up and down a room as if they were answering a bell, and by this agility secure the easiest chair before their seniors have got half-way to them. . . . Already has the ease of the women created insolence in the men. For instance, one of our gentlemen of consequence, after a little rattling conversation with a very pretty girl, said: 'Now if you wish to play I will go and hear you, but you really must get the music I mentioned for 'tis quite a tax on one's patience to listen to such antediluvian stuff as you have here.' Another absurdity which astonishes me is the languid indolence which people assume at times, while at others they are equal to any exertions, except, indeed, those of the mind which seems constantly in a state of inanity; the men talk like cooks or grooms, and the women like chemists. I wish you could induce your fair readers to consider whether the ease of modern days is a good substitute for that dignity which formerly marked the gentlewoman, and whether the depravity of morals may not be traced to the laxity of manners, which in proscribing form and introducing familiarities has smoothed the way to impropriety."

The modern attitude to Marriage is depicted in a letter of 1814:—"I observe with grief and astonishment that marriage is dwindled into a state of contemporary convenience to be continued or dissolved at pleasure. At the nuptials of two opulent young people in our neighbourhood I supposed we should all be expected to attend at church, but the lady gave me to understand that my preparations were unnecessary:

that her father and brother were enough to attend her, and the fewer people to go the sooner their business would be done. At breakfast, accordingly, we met the newly married pair, with looks as serene as though nothing had occurred out of the common. After a hasty but hearty meal, this fashionable couple departed for his seat . . . his old house is to be gutted, altered in every respect and furnished anew. 'We shall not have a room to sit or sleep in, to be sure,' remarked the lady, 'but at Cheltenham or Weymouth or some of those places, accommodation is always to be had.' What can be augured from a commencement of such indifference, where there was even a disregard not merely of ceremony, but of all solemnity?"

Occasionally such criticisms provoked the young woman of the day to retort in a manner which does not suggest that she was given to swoons and sentiment. Such a one, in 1817, addresses the Editress herself, who had expressed disapproval of modern behaviour. ". . . You should recollect that this is an enlightened age, and as I am an advocate for the Rights of Women, I shall take care that no young friend within the sphere of my control shall read your fusty paper, written under the influence of the hip, while you

sit poking over your lamp, taking loads of nasty
snuff and fancying yourself the Queen of Sheba.
Are such as you to decry the spirit of the modern
age? Do you want to prevent the girls from getting husbands by transforming them into such
mumpish things as yourself? I have no doubt of
your being some old devotee, who, having sinned
till you can sin no longer, have given yourself
up to mummery and mortification: torment yourself and everybody about you, and call it reforma-
tion. But shall such things be endured? No! Not
while I can prevent it!"

Truly a dreadful creature. . . . *Cet animal
est très méchant; quand on l'attaque, il se
defend* . . .

One observes that in the Vertical Epoch the
attitude of the ordinary young woman towards
the workings of the sex instinct was unsophisti-
cated. About such matters she was frank, wholesome, but uneducated. She was fully aware of the
dangers of designing villains by whom she might
be undone, but without knowledge of how to
distinguish them; she accepted the system that
marriage was a necessary leap in the dark, and
then, of course, maternity, with its annual risk
of death. . . . Man, in the abstract, a thrilling
Enigma—in the concrete, a Monster, tameable,

even amiable, when disguised in liquor, and, of course, to be a married woman is to have arrived!

She had not envisaged the future beyond that. She was not, as yet, criticising Woman's position in respect to marriage, but in the dimmest fashion at the back of her mind she was starting to wonder about her position as a social being. Bracing ideas were blowing across the Channel, revolutionary phrases about Liberty and Equality; they may, in time, have a meaning for *her*. . . .

As she steps inquiringly into the 19th century, she assumes a bolder air. She starts by discarding her sentiment, and a good deal of her clothing. Inevitably a certain coolness marked the young woman of the Vertical Epoch.

That it was a period of exhibitionism is amply proved by contemporary comments. "What delicate mind can view with unconcern the *nudes* we meet everywhere? The arm, once covered, is now bared nearly to the shoulder, the bosom shamefully exposed, and far more the ankle," was a wail in 1806. The evening dresses of the following year, with "the bosom cut lower in compliment to the back, and shoulders which still continue their public exhibition, braving both moral and physical declamation," provoked an outcry. "The ladies of the first fashion, in order to set all competition at defiance, actually appeared in public more than half naked; but instantly the whole necks, arms, shoulders and bosoms in the kingdom were thrown open to the eye of the gazer. It was but yesterday that I cheapened a pair of gloves with a little damsel who, in point of nakedness, might have vied with any duchess in the land."

Although in the following year we are told that "rouge is going out, and our fair ones are at length content to interest rather than to dazzle," the prevailing habit still provoked a critic to remark —"The monstrous exhibition which some women make of their backs below the scapula is a fashion which sets taste at defiance."

The opposing schools of thought were summarised in a discussion in 1809, when the modern advocate maintained that "the dress of the British Fair shall be established on principles of Nature"; a remark to which an old lady retorted: "Nature, indeed! It would make the ghosts of our grandmothers blush could they see how much of Nature is already exposed! I will write myself to the Bishop of London on the subject."

Thus do desperate ills call for desperate remedies.

However, the flood of exhibitionism began to abate from about 1810, as soon, in fact, as the innate Gothic instincts of the Nation showed signs of recovery; but it continued in a modified form until the end of the epoch, if we may judge from an epigram fired off in 1818:

"When dressed for the evening the girls
    nowadays
Scarce an atom of dress on them leave;
Nor blame them; for what is an evening
    dress
But a dress that is suited for Eve?"

During the period of extreme exhibitionism, it is significant that the headgear and face were made as aggressively noticeable as possible; just as in our own day nudity and face painting go together: a familiar tactical manœuvre, to feign attack on one wing and then to throw forward the centre.

The use of the veil was, in this epoch, much more obviously a weapon of attack, than, as in the Victorian period, a means of defence. It was never of a texture or colour to conceal or distort the features. "The display of bare backs and shoulders," we are informed with some candour, "may be admitted so long as it is confined to a fair young and plump person; and while they are meliorated by the flowing veil, whose sheltering delicacy heightens the beauty which it seeks to veil."

Or, more naïvely in 1804, we are instructed in its strategy: "The present style of dress is the most graceful that can be conceived. The veil suspended from the head and covering the whole figure is a happy device of modesty blended with taste, at a time when, from the shortness of the sleeves and the openness of the robe upon the bosom, delicacy seems to require some protection from the vulgar gaze."

"The light sylphoid forms are entirely exploded; nothing is considered so outré as a slender waist, while the en bon point is the ne plus ultra of feminine proportions."

(It did not occur to them that an even better protection from the vulgar gaze would have been more clothing.)

It may be noted that in those days the generous display did not include the leg; indeed, while en bon point was the ne plus ultra, as a weapon of sex-attraction it might not have been judicious. And being neither flat-chested nor round-shouldered they were not driven by paucity of charms to feature the spikes of their lumbar vertebræ.

While accepting the principles of Nature in the mode of their dress, they were, nevertheless, aware that Nature sometimes admits of improvement, and they were well versed in the methods of doing so. We can learn something on this point from a satirical notice, in a magazine of 1800, professing to advertise a "Register Office for Beauty": "I beg leave to state that I have procured, with infinite labour and expense, the choicest collection of all the several articles for mending, restoring, improving and supplying every female beauty. I have a considerable stock of unguents, cosmetics, and beautifying pastes. I have the finest tinctures to colour the hair, the brightest red salve for foul lips, and the sweetest perfumes for stinking breaths. I shall sell a compound to take off all superfluous hair. I have various shapes ready fitted up, of all sizes, with all sorts of cushions, plumpers, and bolsters to hide any defects. Hairs are plucked out of the forehead and the smoothest Mouse-eyebrows put in. I have a thin diet-drink to bring down the over-plump to a proper gentility of slimness."

The ordinary advertising columns in these magazines for ladies help to throw some light on their inclinations and tastes. They devoted much care to the complexion, employing Wither's "Sicilian Bloom of Youth," Pear's "Liquid Vegetable Rouge," Venus's "Vegetable Bloom," "Cream de Sultanes," Mosenau's "Pomade for colouring the lips," Collicett's "Bloom soap, producing all the effects of Chicken gloves and other preventatives, softening the skin and giving it a most angelic whiteness," each of which, we are assured (by the makers) is unrivalled and all others useless.

Their health and spirits were maintained by incomparable medicines, while "Sloane's Reanimating Pills" were "a Sovereign Remedy for those distressing Debilities which render unhappy the Married State (but cannot, with a due regard to delicacy, be mentioned in a public magazine)." On the other hand, in an advertisement entitled "Lost Happiness Regained" we are informed "Any Female involved in distress from an expectation of inevitable dishonour may obtain consolation and security and meet with motherly attention so necessary on those occasions for the restoration of that serenity of mind attendant on cultivated life," by addressing a line (post-paid) to one Mrs. Grimston, etc.

In the Victorian Magazines for Ladies we

search for such advertisements in vain.

Such, then, were some of the aspects of the women of the Vertical Epoch, as perceived by their contemporaries and betrayed by themselves.

If we examine the fashions of their Dress we see how these too were in harmony with their mental attitudes. The vertical influence survived all through the epoch, but the extreme forms were most marked during the first half; as soon as the mind began to change, so too the style of dress: the pure Classical influence losing its energy and being more and more modified by Gothic notions. The changes are best seen by a table:—

PURE CLASSICAL PERIOD

1800–1803 Classical Form. Classical Ornament.

1804–1807 Classical Form. Egyptian and Etruscan Ornament.

DEBASED CLASSICAL PERIOD

1808–1810 Classical Form. Spanish Ornament.

1811–1813 Debased Classical Form. Slight Gothic Ornament.

1814–1817 Debased Classical Form. Increasing Gothic Ornament.

1818–1821 Diminishing Classical Form. Increasing Gothic Form and Ornament.

The first Gothic signs are in the method of ornament, such as vandyking, gores, puffed hem, flounces, etc.

Later Gothic signs are in the Form, such as an increasing width of skirt and narrowing of the waist producing an angular effect.

In the middle years of the epoch the two modes appear together, and gradually the Classical loses its grip and the Gothic assumes control. Throughout, the vertical line is emphasised by a high waist, producing a disproportionately long skirt which is narrow, hanging at first in loose folds, and later in a stiff tubular form; while transverse lines are suppressed or at least minimised, and angular effects avoided.

The Classical principle that the dress should reveal the beauty of the body is obtained by a paucity of underclothing, and dress materials of a thin transparent texture. In addition, especially at the beginning of the epoch, there was an enthusiasm for exhibitionism; sometimes a substantial area of the back was exposed, sometimes of the bosom, and always the shape of the breasts is emphasised, either by their being pushed up into prominence by mechanical means, or by the lightest of coverings. The arms, even in the day, were often bare to the shoulder. On the other

hand the legs were never exposed, but their outlines indicated by the clinging material of the
dress. The taste for white muslin, especially at
the beginning of the epoch, was to suggest white
marble and ape the effect of a classical statue.

The general effect of the dress was one of
studied simplicity; it aimed at drawing a transparent veil over the allurements of anatomy, and
charmed by revealing everything it concealed.
The supposition that such a style was a reaction
from artificiality is belied by the fact that it was,
in its way, equally artificial and unnatural.
When, indeed, has Woman's dress ever been
otherwise? The headgear was characteristically
arresting both in shape and colour, and the
variety of designs innumerable and incredible. It
was said in 1806 that "A lady is not considered
fashionable if she appears two successive days in
the same bonnet." The face clamoured for attention in bonnets and hats of all shapes and sizes
and colours, and worn at all angles. Indeed every
form which has been worn by Woman since was
invented in the ten years from 1800 to 1810.

That the whole costume was primarily intended
to arrest the eye rather than to protect the wearer
may be deduced from a quotation in 1811: "Some
of our fair dames appear, in summer and winter,

with no other shelter from sun or frost than one single garment of muslin or silk over their chemise—*if they wear one*—but that is dubious, for the chemise is now too frequently banished."

It is an error, however, to suppose that stays were not worn during this epoch; on the contrary, not only were stays constantly advertised but there were frequent references to their use (and abuse). Thus, in 1807: "Stays are in the present style of dress of great importance; long stays have now for a considerable time made part of the female costume." A stay-maker advertises "fifteen patterns of stays, adapted to every size and shape"; while a rival announces that *her* pattern (at four guineas, ready money) "has succeeded in five thousand cases in removing with perfect ease the fullness of the stomach and bowels." In 1810 "long stays are entirely exploded," although there is still a delicate allusion to "the present mode of bracing the digestive portion of the body in what is called Long Stays, with the aid of padding to give shape where there is none; long stays compass into form the chaos of flesh." At this date "the Englishwoman must be at least embonpoint; the bosom must be pushed up by waddings and whalebone; the stays laced as tight as possible over the waist and hips; the excessive compression of those close long stays and iron busks produce diseases too frightful to name."

But in spite of these efforts to improve Nature, there were complaints. Someone writes in 1811: "By the newly invented corsets we see, in eight women out of ten, the hips squeezed into a circumference little more than the waist; and the bosom shoved up to the chin, making a sort of fleshy shelf disgusting to the beholders and certainly most incommodious to the wearer."

During the second half of the epoch the Short Stay was preferred, and for its correct application it is recommended that "the daughter should lie face-downwards on the floor so that her mother, by placing a foot in the small of the back, can thereby obtain a good purchase on the laces."

On the whole, then, we may conclude that the Art of Dress in the Vertical Epoch was not as simple as it looked. We perceive how laborious were the efforts to attain the desired result, to strike the eye of the observer at any cost, ever the ambition of the ardent exhibitionist.

An impression of the women of this period derived solely from Jane Austen's novels is seen to need some amendment; she was, of course, drawing from a small and somewhat unfashionable portion of the community; moreover Miss

Austen's novels do not deal with the most striking part of this epoch; the first half of them were written before 1800, and the rest after 1810. Most of the other novelists of the period were, unfortunately, of an older generation and out of sympathy with the "trend of modern thought." They wrote sentimental and improving works in the vain hope of arresting a movement they deplored.

"Improving novels," however admirable in intention, are seldom trustworthy guides to contemporary life.

The sort of evidence, of which samples have been given, appears to give intrinsic signs of being more reliable, largely because much of it is "circumstantial" in nature.

It indicates that the woman of this epoch was confident in manner and candid in speech; that her feelings were controlled by a shrewd commonsense; that she could relish life without rhapsodising over it, and that she appreciated precisely the ultimate goal to which Instinct was drawing her. There was but one; and she stepped out gaily towards it with an audacious assurance.

Chapter III

The Dawn of Romance

THE years 1821 to 1839 formed a chapter of the 19th century which has been described as "the Romantic Revival," but we can distinguish in it two phases: in the first, the romantic attitude was almost consciously assumed: in the second, it had become almost unconsciously ingrained. It would be convenient, and not unhistorical, to claim that the former occupied, roughly, the '20s and the latter the '30s.

So far as they affected the mentality of the average woman we can detect in them distinct shades of difference. During the one she was acquiring a habit of mind which in the latter had become second nature.

The period of the '20s was one of reconstruction. The whole of Europe had been released from an intolerable burden; the brutal schoolmaster had been packed off to St. Helena, and the schoolchildren, escaping from a term of twenty years, now looked forward to a perpetual holiday.

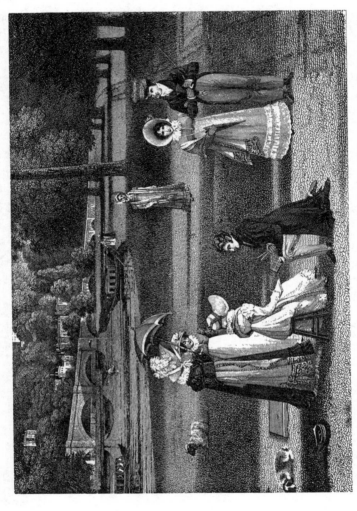

RICHMOND FROM TWICKENHAM PARK. Painted by T. C. Hofland. Engraved by Charles Heath. 1822.

The Dawn of Romance

The first and obvious thing to do was to forget the lessons learnt. The great people who assumed control were busy encouraging a return to the 18th century, while lesser people were equally engaged in personal readjustments. The Englishwoman began to discard many of those disturbing ideas which had been hovering in her mind; the attractive notion of emancipation from her fetters seemed, after all, to be slightly alarming; perhaps she could arrive at her goal by some less obvious route. Instead of aiming to improve her own position, might it not be simpler to improve, if she could, the nature of the male animal whom Providence had, in its infinite wisdom, ordained to be her perpetual superior?

During the first half of the century Woman's position underwent a profound development. In 1800 she had been almost a servant; by 1850 she had become a Perfect Lady. In the '20s she was half-way. It was no longer good manners for the man to behave towards her with the genial coarseness of the 18th century, but it was still the mode to regard her as fair game. He granted her favours, but no rights.

By the middle of the century she was to exchange favours for privileges; the rights were still more distant.

In the 20's she was, of course, unaware of such coming delights; she was, indeed, unconscious of having any deliberate plan behind the tactics she began to adopt. All she was aware of was a surge of feeling which now began to colour her existence and obscure the outlines of reality. For a generation she had schooled herself to be unsentimental, and now the school was shut and done with.

This new and delicious sensation might, therefore, be permitted, nay! encouraged, and thus the desire to perceive was replaced by a desire to feel.

With her instinct for the immediate things at hand it seemed that in her relations to the other sex her emotions could be admirably employed in raising imperceptible barriers behind which she could escape from his world into one of her own fashioning.

Besides, by becoming elusive, would not her charm be still more effective? It was the kind of method which appealed to her feminine instinct. The frank display of the past epoch had, apparently, satiated Man. He had become irresponsive. Perhaps she had been too ready to show her hand—and more; it almost seemed that in spite of her efforts she was still the despised sex; or was it, by chance, because of those efforts? Man, that incomprehensible creature, it seems, grows bored by the obvious; very well, she would henceforth be a Sphinx, and tempt him to discover, if he could, whether or no the Sphinx concealed a secret.

Some vague notion of this sort may have hovered on the edge of her conscious mind, or one may more safely assume she was merely following the whispers of a sagacious instinct.

At any rate, during this period, she appeared to be affecting a strategic retreat from the ground she had won in the former epoch. She surrendered her sceptical attitude, her intellectual interest, the cool frankness of outlook, and the hard masculinity which she had adopted, and instead wove round her personality a romantic web, in the obscurity of which she could wait and watch and conjure visions. . . .

> "And where the red was, lo! the bloodless
>   white,
> And where the truth was, the likeness of a
>   liar;
> And where the day was, the likeness of
>   the night . . ."

In keeping with the new strategy she rapidly

assumed a new fashion of clothing. The vertical line vanished, and with it all that frank physical revelation. If Man would no longer look he should no longer be permitted to see. The Gothic principle of disguise of mind and body was the new mode.

The classical form of the dress with its vertical emphasis of line had already become blurred by Gothic types of ornamentation; but now, in the early '20s, the form itself began to become definitely Gothic, while the classical features were relegated to an occasional odd decoration or so. The shoulder line had widened and the upper sleeve become puffed out; to correct this top-heaviness the base of the skirt was weighted with thick lines of puffing or plastered with foliage-patterns laid on with a heavy hand, so that sometimes the wearer seemed as though she had been wading up to the knees in mud.

It signified something more than mere balance; it was almost ballast. At the same time the waist line fell to the natural level and steadily diminished in diameter, while the skirt steadily widened. From a parallelogram, the outline was approaching that of an hour-glass.

The surface of the dress still bore remnants of classical ornament; perhaps a Greek key-pattern trailing incongruously across a Gothic skirt; or an "Anglo-Greek" bodice, with slanting lines cut short by a pinched waist.

These survivors of an obsolete attitude were choked by vandyking, and scalloping, and scraps which seemed to be the debris of a 14th century church. Crochets and dog-tooth ornaments ran gaily up and down, and "Early English" patterns of blonde lace appeared on neck and sleeves. In addition, a striking change in the colour scheme began to show. Whereas in the Vertical Epoch there had been an inclination to use an intense contrasting colour as ornament on a neutral background, now, in the early '20s, began a taste for sympathetic colours equally distributed. Materials were patterned all over so that at a certain distance the colours would blend. For evening wear, the vogue was for broché silks, for "celestial blue," or pink, lightened by abundance of blonde lace; while for the day, chintz patterns, of three or four mixed colours, were hailed with delight.

Towards the end of the '20s the Gothic victory was absolute; with the immense width of the shoulder line now obtained by Pelerine cape and swollen sleeves, the upper half of the body seemed to be an inverted triangle balanced on a tiny waist, from which the diverging lines of the skirt produced another triangle, apex uppermost.

The enthusiasm for Gothic angles was accentuated by placing on top of this structure an immense hat, embellished by, perhaps, a hundred and twenty feet of parti-coloured ribbons in loops and bows. The whole betokened a growing sense of confidence.

It is not difficult to perceive a richly emotional nature in the wearer of a hat described as "composed of white gauze with lilac ribbons; the strings of ribbons six inches broad, having a white ground bordered with two shades of bright green and sprigs of intense red; ornamented with bouquets of sweet-peas, honeysuckle, red roses, musk and scarlet geranium in their natural colours."

The transformation was now complete. The last trace of the classical spirit had vanished; there was no longer a woman's shape; the romantic creature had retired from view into the recesses of her costume.

And as her body vanished from sight, her mind escaped more and more into a world of fantasy beyond any hope of Man's understanding. In despair he called her the Incomprehensible, as he girded his loins in pursuit. It was an extraordinarily successful manœuvre. That it entailed some physical inconvenience to her must be admitted. The new style of clothing, with its voluminous layers and its corsets, must have been, at first, a severe strain on those brought up in looser days, for by now tight lacing was not merely a mode of the Smart Set, but had become a desideratum of decorum throughout the land.

A letter from a tradesman, in 1828, calls attention to the practice, even in the middling class: "My daughters are living instances of the baneful consequences of the dreadful fashion of squeezing the waist until the body resembles that of an ant. Their stays are bound with iron in the holes through which the laces are drawn so as to bear the tremendous tugging which is intended to reduce so important a part of the human frame to a third of its natural proportion. They are unable to stand, sit or walk, as women used to do. To expect one of them to stoop would be absurd. My daughter, Margaret, made the experiment the other day; her stays gave way with a tremendous explosion, and down she fell upon the ground, and I thought she had snapped in two."

We cannot be surprised at his adding that his daughters "are always complaining of pains in the stomach."

But that was the criticism of a prosaic father on whom feminine subtlety is wasted.

At the same date, among the higher walks of life, "not content with excessive tight lacing our ladies of fashion pad themselves till they resemble bottle-spiders," while the enormous size of the hats was such that an observer "watched a lady sidling with difficulty into Green Park by the narrow Piccadilly gate." Their sleeves, too, had become gigantic, and their buckram linings produced such a rustle that in a drawing-room of ladies, speech was inaudible above the din. Presently it was observed, with regret, that "large sleeves are now so common that they are seen on females of the lower and vulgar class." (A happy arrangement of nature whereby fashions tend to destroy themselves by becoming too common to be any longer a means of attraction.)

In the early '20s fruitless attempts were made to check the new mode. Ladies were implored "to maintain something of the ease and grace attached to the once dominant Grecian costume amongst us, against the newly sprung up Goths and Vandals in the shape of staymakers who have just armed themselves with whalebone and steel to the utter destruction of all native born fine forms."

As though the high-tide of Gothic revival could

be stopped by a letter to a journal.

We must assume that so much physical discomfort could only have been borne by the consciousness of mental satisfaction. Woman's mind was becoming romantic, and her dress was expressing her new mood. And it was precisely the mood by which the man of that day was charmed. Her extraordinary appearance became, to him, a fascinating mystery. He, too, had acquired a distaste for realism; Europe had nearly died under the surgeon's knife and now craved for more soothing treatment. The emotions, which alone make civilisation tolerable, came to the rescue, and everywhere there was reclothing of ideas; Liberty was to mean no more than freedom to obey; Equality was discovered to be a heavenly thought reserved for the next world, and Fraternity—simply, that those with a stake in the country must stick together.

To many it had seemed, at that time, that civilisation itself was tottering to a crash; the Upper Orders were depraved, the Lower Orders insubordinate, and Government helpless. Gradually the new attitude of mind supplied the cure, sentimentalism cheered and slightly intoxicated an exhausted people; they began once more to hope and to pray.

All forms of Art were influenced by the new habit of expressing feeling. The opera "Der Freischutz" seemed charged with a novel form of emotion which was hailed with delight in this country. Byron and Walter Scott led their readers into a vast world of fantasy infinitely more thrilling than realism. Amidst the dullest of domestic surroundings a woman could, at choice, slip into that agreeable dreamland, and become the willing victim of a Corsair, or, by doubling the parts of Minna and Brenda, experience the delicious agitation of being desired by both the pirate and the virtuous hero at the same time. Indeed, by such means, there was nothing to prevent the most virtuous female from indulging in a polygamous fancy to her heart's content.

And the man of that day, he too began once more to attitudinise. Fresh from his ultimate triumph over the Corsican ogre, he felt the need for an outlet for his high animal spirits. His tastes, at least if he belonged to the Best Circles, were simple and somewhat noisy; he drank and gorged and gambled, and had an odd liking for horse-play. If he belonged to less aristocratic stock, he was dull and domineering. In either case it was not very promising material out of which to make a romantic lover. That the woman of that period succeeded in so doing was a remarkable feat. She diffused round herself a halo; she created an Ideal which seemed to impart encouragement; and she saw to it that the illusion was maintained. It was surely the romantic attitude of mind which rescued the nation from its torpor; and in this Woman unconsciously played a large part.

The Art of the country began to express the new philosophy; it was natural that it should move in the direction of a Gothic Revival, but the gap between it and the Classical mode was too wide to be immediately bridged. One detects all sorts of compromising forms between the old and the new, cropping up in the '20s, even in those types of Art which are not the work of genius; the domestic surroundings of the home lost their Classical appearance. The thin-lipped reticence of Sheraton satin-wood expanded into full-bellied mahogany. Appetising pictures of dead game graced the parlour walls, while in the drawing-room, portraits of Abraham and Moses in coloured silks supplied an awful reminder of higher things—a symbol, as it were, of the British taste for plenty of food and a little religion. In fact, the nation was beginning to feel itself again.

It had not yet become smug; prosperity was still in the future; but it was becoming confident, and therefore turgid.

If, in our attempt to reconstruct the mentality of the woman of the period, we turn to the magazines dedicated to their use, we find some striking changes since the former Epoch.

They have lost much. Gone, alas! are those columns of "news of the month," with their luminous details. It appears that it was no longer considered nice for innocent virgins to read accounts of actual ravishments; for them it was now more satisfactory to be ravished by deputy, as it were, in fictitious tales of love, so that they might obtain the perpetual enjoyment of both having their cake and eating it—or, at least, nibbling at it.

Gone, also, are the philosophic essays and scientific articles; such information might be disturbing to the well-ordered mind, and impart ideas.

A veil of propriety is now drawn over the "facts of nature," although occasionally one may light upon something which seems to have been accidentally left over from the old, out-spoken days. Thus, in 1828, a ladies' magazine of the highest principles narrates a drawing-room dialogue between two mothers, while their respective daughters are just out of earshot.

" 'I suppose,' said her ladyship, in allusion to Mrs. Buckle's condition, 'you expect soon?'

" 'Hush!' she replied, drawing nearer, 'speak lower, if you please, when Rosa is in the room; she is so innocent, dear girl! She actually believes that all her little brothers and sisters are found under the cherry tree. It is so very delightful to have their minds such perfect white paper . . .' "

Meanwhile, at the other end of the room Laura is remarking to Rosa: " 'So, Rosa, I see Mrs. Buckle is in the family way again.'

" 'Hush, Laura, pray speak lower, for Mama thinks I don't know anything about it. Our old Nurse and Sally always tell me everything, but Mama would be so angry if she knew. I heard her one day advise Lady Blaney never to let her girls have the run of the library, so the first day Papa was out I got into the study to see what the reason could be, and I'm sure I never read so much in my life as I did that afternoon. But la! there was nothing but what everybody knows. Mama is always so afraid even of my brothers seeing "Reece's Medical Guide"; I took down a book all about physic, just to know why we may not see it, but just as I was opening "Metaphysics" I heard a footstep; it seemed to be all about some horrid disorder; I saw the word "matter" so often. I don't know where the complaint is.'

" 'No more do I,' said Laura, 'but I believe it is only a disorder in the head. . . .' "

As a compensation for these omissions the magazines provide a wealth of fiction. There are adventures with Arab sheikhs, into whose clutches the heroine falls, fierce fascinating Othellos, whose illicit passions—at the critical moment—are curbed by the contemplation of the virtues of the victim (but, of course, the reader can skip that bit and let her imagination wander. . . .). There are mysterious heroes who turn out to be members of the Aristocracy . . . but whether the male protagonist be a black man or a peer, in each case his coarser nature is subdued by the refining influence of the female. The hypothesis is emphasised; Man's destiny is to be civilised by Woman: such is her obvious rôle. The task of civilising herself is postponed. We must suppose that this kind of story not merely expressed the attitude of the readers, but even helped to form its finer shades. Young women would come to accept such a belief as not merely pleasant but probable, for with popular journalism there is always the chance that it may be believed.

After a prolonged perusal of these magazines a vision of the ideal hero emerges: "His visage was gloomy, yet engaging; the dark traits of his countenance hung like the lowering clouds of the brooding storm till enlivened by a ray of sunny sweetness. A large raven-tinted eye shone beneath the canopy of a deep brow, depicting in its gaze the mystic workings of an elevated mind." We are not surprised to learn that "he is imbued by the conscious thought that in all his afflictions his heart has never swerved from rectitude." It was, perhaps, a little hard on the ordinary man, having to approach a young lady who had been immersed in this. Can we blame him for becoming, in his turn, a little turgid?

A type of story, which has some psychological significance, begins to appear about this date. The following, although perhaps not of the highest order of literature, deserves attention. We are introduced to "a tall, handsome young man, though too slender and pale even to sickliness. His features were marked with premature lines which bespoke a troubled heart." He is in love, but "his spirits instead of mending in her society grew worse and worse; he always returned much dejected and sometimes so agitated that he would drink glass after glass of pure brandy to recover his self-possession." For, in fact, he was wedded to another. "Mary is an angel! How little does she think that I have found too late the being whom Nature intended for me, and am writhing in the shackles which hold me from her!" He does the correct thing: goes out into the snow-storm, where, later, he is discovered "with his teeth clenched and his countenance exhibiting an expression of sullen despair; but death had already borne him away to his rest."

Observe, it is the man who dies of despair while the female Angel survives in triumph. It will be found in the '40s that the formula becomes reversed, but in the romantic '20s the woman had not yet acquired a full appetite for masochism. But this taste for psychological triumph over the male was not allowed to develop without protest from the elder generation who still tried to teach the young that it is a woman's lot to suffer. We can detect the hand of an elder in the sad story of Edith who "was devotedly attached to her parents and seldom failed in obedience to their requests," until alas! a gentleman appeared whose mind "was as depraved as his exterior was fascinating." We are told in plain words that "though he was resolved to win her love he had no intention of leading her to the altar. Oh! Ye despoilers of female innocence! However ye may laugh in your fancied security and boast of your triumphs, be assured the day is coming when sickness and death shall overtake you and ye shall tremble to think of that awful tribunal to which ye are hastening!" Edith elopes and is abandoned. "Sin ever carries with it its own punishment. No ermined robe can prevent the corroding worm from preying on the heart beneath!" At least the author says so, although it seems a harsh description of an unborn baby, even an illegitimate one. Fortunately the baby dies, and Edith sinks into a well-deserved decline. In fact, "her gentle spirit quits its earthly tenement. Oh! Happy is that female who, by the purity and correctness of her behaviour pursues the path of virtue and saves the hearts of her parents from witnessing the disobedience and disgrace of their daughter!"

We must suppose from the reiteration of this plot in various forms that the warning was needed in that generation.

Suspicious, too, are those petulant comments on the Modern Woman, which are so prone to be uttered by those who are no longer quite modern.

"There is something unfeminine in independence. It is contrary to Nature and therefore it offends. A really sensible woman feels her dependence; she does what she can but she is conscious of her inferiority and therefore grateful for support."

It is unfortunate that the magazines of that period no longer published "letters from correspondents"; whether the young ladies did not write, or editors would not publish, we do not know, but we must assume from the silence that either there was no murmur, or else that it was considered wise to stifle it. Deprived of this direct evidence, we are driven to rely on circumstantial, and the modern student is compelled to read a generous number of these magazines even if he denies himself the delight of perusing the columns of poetry poured into their pages. But in addition to the magazines for ladies, of which the number and size were steadily increasing, there were also the novels. In the year 1826, for example, 250 new novels appeared. To the modern reader the number may not seem so very alarming, but in those days a novel was generally a formidable affair in three or four volumes, and it was customary to read it right through. It would be improper to judge their quality by the few which have survived from that period; indeed beyond the later works of Scott and Peacock it would not be easy, on the spur of the moment, to recall their names; for our purpose it is not the novel written for all time that is so instructive, but rather the novel of the moment. The worse the author the more valuable his work; and it seems that the '20s were richly supplied with authors unhampered by genius, whose novels therefore reflect nothing but the tastes of their readers. In every sense they are invaluable.

An admirable specimen, which deserves to be more widely known, is *The Mysterious Marriage, or the Will of my Father*, by Catherine Ward, 1824. The heroine possesses "a pure angelic countenance which is wont to light up with a melancholy smile; she conducted herself with great fortitude as became a female of sense, by endeavouring to check that excess of sensibility which on some occasions she had strongly indulged in, the only fault (if it be a fault) she was possessed of; but with all her virtues, all the purity of her character and the chaste principles of her disposition, and with a heart as innocent as our frail nature can possibly be gifted with, was yet a woman—and in love; we must forgive her for it; it is not in mortals to be perfect; in this earthly state of our existence we can only endeavour to become so."

There in a single sentence (albeit a somewhat long one) the author has depicted the Model Young Woman of that day.

We cannot be surprised that she does not surrender herself at the altar until after the passage of some six hundred and fifty pages.

Even the reviewers in their notices aimed at inculcating the same high principles. Of a woman novelist (now unfortunately forgotten) we are told that "she teaches the passions to move at the command of virtue. The emotions which her narrative excites are favourable to the best principles of our nature, and tend to refine the soul and purify the heart."

It is impossible to view so much smoke without suspecting the presence of fire, and if we search in other directions we discover similar signs of emotional unrest. A reviewer, commenting on a book of "Winter Evening Pastimes," remarks that "this volume dwells too much upon kissing, and thus tends to render that favour habitual which a lady ought to grant with delicate parsimony and modest reluctance." We find contemporary efforts to trace this excess of sensibility to its cause. One observer, contemplating the Modern Young Woman of his day, exclaims: "What are these lovely young ladies fit for but to dance, sing and play the piano, to dress, take their pleasure, in short to kill time in all the frivolous amusements of the town? Who can, without horror, contemplate all these dire effects resulting from this new-fangled plan of female education?"

Sagacious observer! How near to the mark would have been the diagnosis if only he had added that education is what we learn out of school. . . . For in school the young lady was trained in the most elegant accomplishments: the harp, the pencil and brush, dancing, embroidery, even caligraphy. The results were viewed, at least by some, with a good deal of satisfaction. "Within the last twenty years there has been a great and obvious improvement in female education. Accomplishments are now profusely taught and the minds of young females are expanded and ameliorated."

The ultimate purpose of this education is clearly indicated: "The peculiar province of Woman is to tend with patient assiduity around the bed of sickness; to watch the feeble steps of infancy; to communicate to the young the elements of knowledge, and bless with their smiles those of their friends who are declining in the vale of tears."

The policy which should govern their adult life is depicted with equal clarity: "To improve the present time must be the object of our immediate care, and we must first obtain the necessary influence, by the constant and vigilant cultivation of virtue before we can indulge the benevolent hope that the good seed we have sown will flourish. The most important consideration of the married woman is the discharge of her duty as a wife. It is not easy to number in how many ways a wife may benefit the mind and habits of her husband. He may unhappily be devoid of religious principles; he may be addicted to some vice; may be intemperate or licentious, but the judicious exertion of his wife's influence may produce an amendment."

The young woman of the '20s certainly had a policy put before her with abundance of good advice. We are chiefly interested, however, in ascertaining the results. We have been told what she thought she was like; we have been told what she ought to be like. In reality, what was she?

That she gave the reins to her fancy and cultivated romantic attitudes is evident. It was said that the observance of the Sabbath was being more attended to than it had been formerly; an emotional religion offered an appropriate appeal.

It was no longer merely a matter of decorum; the woman discovered that religion could be transformed into a personal romance for the worshipper. She pictured a Deity regarding her with special interest, and her visits to church had almost the flavour of an assignation with God.

It is impossible to separate the romantic mind from the basal instinct of sex; it will colour the woman's relations with animate and inanimate things, so that she will detect an attractive masculinity in an object or idea, and fall in love with personalities unseen. Indeed she is incapable of feeling a profound interest unless it is tinged with sex emotion, but she skilfully conceals from her mind any such relationship. It would spoil the picture.

With a mind so tuned she faced the incongruities of life, very conspicuous in the '20s. There was the Man of her day; he needed idealising before he could be loved, and sometimes it was not easy to do so. There was the social state round her, its greed and its poverty, and its brutal humour. That too demanded some distortion before the vision could be endured, so she discovered that it was all designed by Providence for a good but obscure purpose. There was her own individual future, and the inevitable things that happen to one of her sex; that background, too, could be concealed from the conscious mind by a process of re-focusing; let the foreground blaze with rich colours . . . and look not beyond. . . . So she learnt to ignore large realities, and cultivated passionate enthusiasms for the trivial.

Her attitude towards Man was changing. Although she seemed to have retired, it was not a defeat but a skilfully conducted change of front. Nor did she wait until the foe chose to make his advances. That may be the attitude of passive sentimentality such as we find in the '40s. But in the '20s she was not yet a lady in the full Victorian sense. She had, perhaps, ceased to be enquiring, but she had not become meek. She boldly displayed her veiled attractions in unfamiliar shape, and flaunted her coloured attitudes of mind, forcing the man to climb emotional heights until his head was turned. She affected to belong to a world outside the masculine sphere of comprehension, playing on his imagination until he came to believe it.

And by the '30s she had come to believe it herself.

Chapter IV

The Romantic '30s

THE efforts, occupying the '20s, to restore
the defunct principles of the 18th century,
were doomed to failure. Everyone, except perhaps the governing class, had moved forward.
If the ideas bred from the French Revolution
were now recognised to be dangerous, the feelings which were growing could not be held back
indefinitely. The sense of irritation grew until
explosions occurred; in France another revolution; in England a Reform Bill, expedients
characteristic of each country.

Here, the demands of the lower orders were
met by giving votes to the middle class, and
liberty to colonial slaves.

It was agreed, early in the '30s, that at last
the 18th century had expired, and that a new era
was about to open; some apprehended chaos,
while the more sanguine foretold perennial peace
and prosperity. The nation paused to survey the
outlook, but without any defined ideas. There

was, instead, a strong romantic feeling affecting the whole social state except the mute labourer who found it difficult to cultivate romantic attitudes on 8/- a week. However, the aristocratic landowner was comforted by the Corn Laws, the merchant by machinery, and the middle class by political power. Prosperity was once more in view, and as a dog will slobber at the sight of a bone, England began to salivate sentiment. We can't help, under such circumstances, our feelings gushing forth, as we search for objects deserving our pity, or, better still, our reprobation. In the early '30s there began that long series of moral attitudes, in which we indulged for the rest of the century, to the bewilderment of the foreigner, who cannot allow for our fits of inebriation. He will attribute to hypocrisy what is, after all, only moral insobriety. As a relief to our feelings we are apt, at such times, to break out into religious revivals. There is an overwhelming desire to substitute picturesque ideals for harsh reality; hence the Oxford Movement, beginning in 1833; the same psychological impulse that led the young woman of that day to intoxicate her mind with romantic fiction, inspired Newman's to soar into a realm of spiritual fantasy. For him the Lives of the Saints as he

fettered his soul in mediævalism: for her the
novels of Scott as she tightened her stays.

Newman's dislike of realism, although it took
an unpopular form, was characteristic of the English attitude of the time.

The Oxford Movement affected a small section
of the community, but a similar refining influence
spread through all branches of religious thought;
the high and dry Tory parson, the Low Church,
the Nonconformist, all stirred themselves according to their lights to improve their forms of
appeal. A sort of spring-cleaning of the creeds
took place; the gloom of Hell was less stridently
advertised; Heaven was made, if possible, even
more attractive than it had been.

It was, of course, still the narrow theology of
a century ago, which then was accepted as
religion, but it was definitely attempting to throw
off the coldness of the 18th century. Religion
was becoming less forbidding, sometimes supplying even comfort instead of terror. Certainly it
was expressing more intense feeling. And by this
change it was increasing its influence on women.

But religion was also being employed, beyond
its legitimate scope, as a means of social
propaganda.

We discover an enormous increase in the

number of "religious" and "improving" works, especially those designed to mould the characters of the young, and a study of the writings of Mrs. Ellis, Esther Copley, Anna Marie Sargeant, Mrs. Sherwood, and similar authors, reveals that, instead of spiritual training, a steady pressure was being put upon the rising generation to check enquiry or even thought; that proper subordination to authority was the real lesson taught by them, the object being to eradicate any traces of that emancipatory movement which had been visible at the beginning of the century.

The girl of the middle and upper classes was now being trained in a strict discipline; she was taught to "believe" in order that she might learn to obey. The effect of this system on a highly romantic nature produced an attitude of mind still more noticeable in the next decade, but towards the end of the '30s we can detect Romanticism subsiding into a vapid Sentimentalism. It is remarkable that there was no counter-movement. At the moment we are chiefly concerned with the initial steps leading to this change.

To what sort of training was the girl of the '30s subjected? As regards her mind, we cannot do better than quote the advice given by Esther

Copley in her *Female Instructor*. The Young Person is urged to utter a morning prayer (occupying a page and a half) containing the pious remark, "O Lord, I am a sinner. Behold, I was shapen in iniquity, and in sin did my mother conceive me."

In spite of this reflection upon her mother, implicit obedience to the wishes of her parents is insisted on; she must, without pause, study the moral significance of every experience, and acknowledge the loving hand of the Lord in every misfortune. Even in her amusements she must observe Satan at her elbow, and she must be ever searching her heart for sinful thoughts, and hastily eradicate them. Is not the heart of Man above all things deceitful and desperately wicked? As for the heart of Woman. . . . Here Mrs. Ellis, writing at the end of the decade, when we should have supposed that ten years' discipline would have produced at least some improvement, has a distressing confession to make. "The women of England are deteriorating in their moral character, and false notions of refinement are rendering them less influential and less happy than they were." She ascribes it to the fatal practice of cultivating the mental faculties in preference to the moral. "By far the greater proportion of the young ladies (for they are no longer *women*) of the present day are distinguished by a morbid listlessness of mind and body, and a constant pining for excitement and an eagerness to escape from everything like practical and individual duty."

She adds: "The number of languid, listless and inert young ladies who now recline upon sofas is to me a melancholy spectacle; it is but rarely that we meet with a really healthy woman."

Mrs. Ellis attributed this lamentable state of things to over-education, and no doubt she was right if we understand by that term the disciplining processes already referred to.

The moulding was converting a full-blooded romanticism into an anæmic sentimentalism.

That the transformation was not accepted entirely without murmur by its victims may be assumed from Mrs. Ellis's admission that "one of the most striking features in the character of the young ladies of the present day is the absence of contentment; they are lively when excited but no sooner does the excitement cease than they fall back into their habitual listlessness, under which they complain of their fate and speak of themselves as unfortunate and afflicted, that one would suppose them to be victims of adversity did not a more intimate acquaintance with their actual circumstances convince us that they were surrounded by everything conducive to rational comfort. It is an undeniable improvement in modern education that religious instruction is becoming more general; so long, however, as this discontent remains so prevalent we must question the sufficiency of this method."

Unfortunately Mrs. Ellis is not very clear in her suggestions for an alternative treatment; in spite of the religious instruction provided in such generous abundance young ladies would persist in going off into a decline.

For it seems that converting young women into young ladies impaired their health. It was now that consumption began to grow fashionable, together with swoonings, anæmia, and various forms of debility.

A good complexion was considered hardly ladylike; an interesting pallor was the mode, implying a romantic disposition.

To obtain it an excellent method was the drinking of strong vinegar, and the eating of large quantities of chalk, but it was advised that the remedies should be taken at different times lest they should combine inside with explosive results.

By such means the stigma of rude health could be removed. A delicate appetite was much preferred, and young women might be forced to nibble scraps in their bedroom so that they could face the dinner-table with ladylike anorexia.

In addition, tight-lacing on a drastic scale was very helpful. To secure the exquisite shape demanded by social convention an early start was necessary, and the schoolgirl was broken in by the use of the backboard, to which her shoulders were strapped for varying periods of time, together with stays having iron busks down the front, and shoulder straps tightly maintaining the correct attitude.

A book entitled *Female Beauty* (1837) remarks that "when indeed corsets are employed to render the chest as small below and as broad above as possible, and greatly to increase the fullness and prominence of the bosom, when the young lady spends a quarter of an hour in lacing her stays as tight as possible, and is sometimes seen by her female friends pulling hard for some minutes, next pausing to breathe, then resuming the task with might and main, till after perhaps a third effort she at last succeeds and sits down covered with perspiration, then it is that the effect of stays is not only injurious to the shape but is calculated to produce the most serious consequences."

The authoress recommends "The Complete Corset" (of which, it seems, she is the maker) which is guaranteed to "support the figure without diminishing the freedom of motion, and to conceal the size of the abdomen when it becomes disproportionately large, either from corpulence or from accidents which naturally occur."

It appears, however, that a large number of young ladies, in spite of these hygienic precautions, developed spinal curvature, and it was suggested by the Faculty that too frequent playing of the harp was the probable cause, and that it might be prevented either by less harp or more stays. There were, of course, some irregular practitioners who held unorthodox views, and one of them, a certain Mr. Donald Walker, ventured to urge that more physical exercise was all that was needed. He published (in 1837) a book, *Exercises for Ladies,* in which he remarks that "Few young ladies are exempt from some degree of deformity, and that a good carriage is better obtained by exercising the body than by the use of the backboard, shoulder straps, collars, or even steel plates"—but, of course, quacks will say anything. . . .

He invented a ladylike form of Indian club and described a series of exercises "which are neither frivolous nor severe, and which are calculated to bestow strength and activity, and to preserve beauty and health." He supplied elegant names for each; thus, the waving of a leg in the air is called "Battemens," of which there appear to be three kinds: Grands battemens: petits battemens: and battemens on the instep. He urged that they should be carried out before meals, and scorning the confines of the bedroom, recommended the middle of an open field for their performance. Mr. Walker disapproved of horse-riding which "produces in ladies a coarseness of voice, a weathered complexion, and unnatural consolidation of the bones of the lower part of the body, ensuring a frightful impediment to future functions which need not here be dwelt upon; by over-development of the muscles equitation produces an immense increase in the waist and is, in short, altogether masculine and unwomanly." For other reasons dancing is also to be avoided. "There are several dances that should be abandoned by delicate women on account of their causing too violent emotions; vertigo is one of the great inconveniences of the waltz; and the characters of this dance, the clasping of the partners, their exciting contact, and the too quick and too long continued succession of agreeable emotions produce sometimes in women of irritable constitutions syncopes, spasms, and other accidents." In fact, the only safe form of exercise is that propounded by Mr. Walker. But his seems to have been a voice crying in the wilderness a century too soon, and even to-day—alas!—we seldom witness the spectacle of young ladies performing, in the wide open spaces, grands battemens on an empty stomach.

Most of Mr. Walker's contemporaries preferred stays and dancing. A ball was a rare event; once or twice in the year a young woman might experience the delicious thrill, and decorously move through a waltz, to the music of Johann Strauss, a galop, the quadrilles, and perhaps a country dance at the end. But most of her time was spent with those of her own sex; she had abundance of sisters with whom she could quarrel over potential beaux (and every young man was that or nothing), but her opportunities of mixing with the other sex were few and carefully guarded. In Miss Eden's *The Semi-attached Couple*, the heroine hesitates to walk down the garden path with a male guest unless accompanied by a chaperone; it would have been unmaidenly, an adventure like stepping into a lion's cage, and one never knows—the beast may be hungry. . . . That, at least, would have been the correct attitude for the young lady of the upper class.

If of the middle class, the conventions were less exacting, but opportunities less frequent, for much of her time was spent indoors performing the task of maidservant, cook, housekeeper, sempstress, under-nurse, and governess combined.

If of higher rank, her leisure was occupied in acquiring those accomplishments which combined gracefulness and absence of intellectual effort. In the main it was the art of attitudinising.

There was, of course, for each class, an opportunity for stimulating the imagination by novel-reading. Of the novels that were read we can deduce the nature from a contemporary criticism of one: "When we say that a novel can be read aloud to a female audience we give it high praise; and if any person be worried in temper or afflicted in thought he will find half a dozen of its chapters a powerful prescription to restore him to himself."

We are not told the effect of reading the whole three volumes.

As a rival to the three-volume novel were the

magazines for ladies, which, in the '30s, were becoming more refined in tone, and more moral in purpose. The stories in them betray the powder in the jam, in spite of their being so very jammy. It is scarcely necessary to read through a story which informs us, in its final line: "Her parents lived to see their daughter a Countess, and what is infinitely better, an exemplary Christian". . . . Ex pede Herculem. . . .

We learn the correct attitude a young lady should adopt towards a potential lover: "In some natures the poetry of love is the very essence of its nature, and for a lover to say: 'Will you have me, yea or nay,' would be so Gothic and barbarous that no young lady's nerves of 18 to 24, could be expected to bear it." If she were to be brought suddenly face to face with a fact, such as a proposal, she might, or at least should, swoon into unconsciousness.

Even agreeable facts were to be viewed through a halo, and disagreeable ones must not be admitted to exist. For the rest of the century that attitude was destined to survive, in which the well-bred girl was so trained that she perceived only selected phenomena, and that her feelings flowed only along acceptable channels.

It was an alternative to becoming civilised. It

chimed in with the standard of moral elevation which was demanded of his women-folk by the Man of the '30s, who had no intention of allowing them to become his rivals, preferring them out of the way on a pedestal, from which they must not descend. His view is admirably expressed by the hero of a story, who remarks to the heroine: "Happy and charming I am sure you are only while you are innocent; for a knowledge of evil, even though it guard from a participation in it, leaves a stain on the purity of the female mind."

In a word, to be perfectly pure, the female mind must be perfectly blank. How such a mind was to be occupied in its leisure hours without impairing its blankness, is frequently discussed in the more thoughtful of the ladies' magazines. One recommends that "conchology is a study peculiarly suited to ladies; there is no cruelty in the pursuit, the subjects are so brightly clean, so ornamental to a boudoir." From another we obtain a precise definition of what a lady should be: "She is a being of delicate perceptions, tremblingly alive to the least infringement of decorum; ever studying to please by unostentatious candour and heartfelt benevolence, anxious to make all around her easy and happy,

polite without ceremony, modest without bashfulness, commanding all sorts of attention by her
retiring and unasking lowliness, and with a
humble, heartfelt piety."

Such, at least, was the standard which Men
desired Women to attain.

One may suspect a similar propagandist effort
in the story of Emilia, who rejects her lover's proposal in these noble phrases: "Hold, Henry, I
have said I will not wed without my father's sanc-
tion; my attachment to you—alas!—is, I must
confess, great; but it must not outweigh my duty
to those who brought me into the world. Go, my
Henry, you will meet with others whose society
will amply compensate for the loss of mine."

That, we can be sure, is how a father in the
'30s would have wished his daughter to behave.

If the magazines of this period are studied, not
so much for their literary excellence as for their
psychological significance, certain features stand
out. The formula of the Female triumphing over
the despairing Male is being given up; and the
Betrayed Damsel returning repentant to the
parental hearth is getting scarce; neither seemed
quite ladylike. Or perhaps, though the hearth was
still there, the Damsel lacked enterprise.

In their place was Virtue triumphing over Vice

(aided by advice from the Proper Source), and Cinderella in suitable forms played at her perennial day-dream. Morality, with scarcely a rag of disguise, stalks through the volumes, while Religion bludgeons a path that none can miss. Such works had the obvious design of making their readers good, but not critical, for problems are never presented, but only stereotyped solutions.

There are, too, picturesque descriptions of foreign lands, and emotional appeals on behalf of the inhabitants of those unchristian regions. You are invited, not to aid, but to sympathise with the down-trodden. Passive feeling is all that is suitable for elegant females.

If we look farther, and examine contemporary memoirs, and those works of fiction which are still famous, we perceive that life was being accepted by women as a romantic picture, tinged with humour and piety. It had ceased to be drama, but had become a panorama. In all the novels of that period the heroine is entirely passive; she looks on as life sweeps by her, bringing joy or misfortune, which she meekly accepts. We may suppose the popular novelist was depicting a popular type, and we must conclude that it was a common one in real life. We see a young woman, with intense feelings but no critical faculty, who never makes the slightest effort to deflect the flow of circumstance.

Every source of information that was open to the young woman of that time reiterated the same teaching; what effect would this steadily applied force have on a creature so malleable that she can be shaped as you wish? That with her infinite adaptability she fitted herself into the surroundings provided may be assumed, and it only needs to measure the shape of the container to know the shape of the contents. The shape Man was designing for her was obvious.

He wanted her to be sedately charming, submissive and innocent, and equipped to perform what he did not care to do himself, such as making him comfortable and producing his children. To do him justice, he was not unwilling to supply what was needed for these purposes.

But there were regions of her mind beyond his reach—indeed, beyond his desire to understand. She drifted through her life, one half of her being occupied with petty matters, the shape of a bonnet, the making of a dish, the perpetual need to humour him whom she had sworn to love, honour and obey: while the other half wandered through fantastic worlds of feeling, groping for the shadow of a hero, or reaching out to bliss denied her, with vague longings for the might-have-been.

For she perceived that whatever Providence had given her, it was not of her own making; so she accepted, without impious questioning, the numerous blessings poured upon her.

There were few signs of discontent; she was completely protected, and she was easily satisfied. She was still capable of relishing the coarser humours of life, for refinement had not yet become ingrained. Her simple practical existence produced a shrewd common sense after the romantic visions of youth had faded. She was efficient for her limited functions, and studied her Man's appetites, for which sole purpose, indeed, the Almighty had created her.

If circumstances permitted she was beginning to call herself a lady, for it had some advantages. It denoted a comfortable cleavage from the stratum below, and justified display, but it did not yet denote the frigid isolation from jolly vulgarity. She had her "company manners," but in private she was not clean. Such was the matron of those days. Her daughter lacked, of course, her experience; in its place she had her romantic attitudes which shielded her from reality: an odd preparation for life, but it seems to have answered.

Even after marriage the two sexes lived in worlds remote from each other. They shared common interests, but not thought, for the more secret regions of their minds were kept apart. To appreciate the coming Victorians properly we have to recognise that this aloofness was growing more marked. The sexes became more incomprehensible to each other ; they were beginning to live in different worlds.

We should expect to find some expression of this attitude of mind to show itself in the clothing, and all through the '30s the Fashions indicate a gradual softening, until towards the close of the decade a sweet prettiness is attained, suggestive of a Sunday doll. The exuberance of the early '30s, with those mammoth sleeves and arresting hats, has subsided, and by '35 the sleeve is shapely once more, with a mere fullness at the elbow, while the bodice skilfully betrays the form in a thousand varieties of mute appeal. In spite of the constraining corsets beneath there seems no stiffness about the dress; the waist is as tight as tugging can make it, and asks for the support of a strong masculine arm; the skirt, short enough to reveal a well-turned ankle, is growing ample but not heavy, for butterfly materials, gaily coloured, suggest a tripping habit. Nevertheless a multiplicity of embroidered petticoats guard the wearer from undue activity. The art of the shawl is studied; it produces entrancing attitudes, and its proper arrangement denotes social breeding. By such means a woman offers a kaleidoscope of poses. But it is the bonnet, after all, that matters in the '30s, and is woman's weapon of attack or defence, for the scuttle-shape, with huge sides flying from the face, displays as much as she chooses of the sparkling eye, the coy ringlets and the romantic pallor of the cheek: or by deft movement, it can shield the wearer from too bold a scrutiny! Its shape seems to indicate a desire to be looked at rather than to look, yet feigns to obstruct the observer. The mixed colours are borrowed from the garden, and blend harmoniously; in the evening, shoulders gleam from a dress cut to reveal as much as modesty dare; a fine shape, slightly stereotyped by corsets, is admitted, but not announced, as though she would disclaim responsibility for its effect.

When cloaked for out-of-doors she assumes a shape of extreme coyness. The exaggerated breadth of the cape and the loose cloak hanging in great masses around her, produce a shortened

—even dumpy—effect, as she scuttles along the road, for it is fashionable to be plump and diminutive in stature. She can always look up to the man at her side.

She is acquiring the art of presenting a picture instead of a person, and pictures are meant to be looked at; we do not expect them to be very informative.

It must be admitted that if we venture to explore beneath the surface we discover that the apparent simplicity was not as complete as it appeared to the masculine eye. The ladies' magazines are too refined to betray secrets, but the book *Female Beauty* is a useful traitor. We are informed that those who wear "very tight stays complain that they cannot sit upright without them, many are compelled to wear night stays when in bed." Demi-corsets, some 8 or 10 inches high, with light whalebones, were worn in the mornings, enabling the wearer to perform domestic duties; when arrayed in her best she bent at her peril. We are also informed that "many persons endeavour to increase their size by aid of a considerable quantity of drapery. Size does, in effect, give a sort of dignity and majesty to the figure, but this may be carried to an excess, as in the extreme enlargement of the hips by means of monstrous bustles, than which nothing can be more ridiculous, not to say indecent. When the bust is too long the defect is concealed by the fullness of the petticoats, supported by a small bustle behind. Nothing, however, can be in worse taste than the monstrous and ill-shaped bustles we commonly see sometimes placed altogether on one side; and sometimes so irregular that they look as if some domestic utensil were fastened under the dress." (Which would, no doubt, produce a jerry-built effect.) From another source we learn that the bustle "has the drawback of being liable to slip out of place, being situated in a region on which the fair wearer is unable to keep an observant eye."

It was her boast that she never leant back in a chair; but, in truth, she could not and dared not.

We are informed that "the wide, flowing petticoats which women wear are generally sufficient to conceal any slight deformity in the shape of the limbs; the existence of such defects can then be surmised only from their style of walking, which requires great attention." That such secrets of the toilet were successfully concealed from the male observer is to be concluded from the absence of any reference to them in general

literature, whereas in the '70s and '80s the bustle
was a matter for public jest.

It was a rule that underclothes, except such
parts as might be visible, were of the plainest
description, as though invisible beauty was not
worth while. Immense pains were taken over anything that might serve to attract the masculine
eye, but there was no innate love of beautiful
things for their own sake; they were but a means
to an end.

The costume was attuned to the mental attitude of the wearer: coy but not demure: innocent
looking but not artless. It appeared to guarantee
the existence of charms which it concealed, and
appealed for admiration without demanding it.
Withal it exhibited grace in restrained movement,
and did not disguise physical gifts and
potentialities. But its form was growing more
and more mysterious. Those triangular Eves with
their romantic airs and tantalising reticences,
their innocence, playful, perhaps artful, were
becoming inscrutable.

Or, at least, it was gentlemanly to think so.
The men were enraptured but did not attempt
to understand them. The Gothic disguise worked
like a charm.

CHAPTER V

The Sentimental '40s

THE '40s present one of those paradoxical
epochs which could be described as either a
time of growing prosperity or of hideous poverty:
of blundering statesmanship or of great reforms:
of rapid advances or of social torpor, according
to the bias of the observer.

Fortunately for us it is not necessary to combine these conflicting views into one homogeneous
whole; we are chiefly concerned with the effect
of the period on the feminine mind.

But we have to recognise the diverse influences
brought to bear upon that mind from various
quarters, economic, social, moral, educational
and religious. As a more or less passive spectator
a woman might have noticed something of the
turmoil going on round her; her feelings might
have been touched by sights not entirely hidden
from her eyes, or she might have felt gratification
at the social improvement in her particular circle;
but it is improbable that she was fully aware of

all the forces remoulding the social state, and it is extremely unlikely that she appreciated fully her own immense significance as one of them.

She seemed a passive spectator; unconsciously she was an active protagonist, perhaps the chief, and the sole force she employed was her super-abundance of feelings.

The sentimental Gothic spirit of the nation was in the ascendant. When we refer to the "Victorian Gothic" period it is to the '40s that we turn to find the most typical examples, and not merely in architecture or furniture design; the notion that Reality could and should be disguised by forms serving no other purpose than as a decent veil over ugly Truth, was the essence of it. It explained the desire to make a railway station resemble a church (which is not only prettier but more moral); supplied an air of holiness to the dining-room furniture, and transformed a mere picture into a lesson. It inspired Ruskin to demand that factories should be made as unlike factories as possible, and Pugin to see that true Faith could be expressed only by a pointed arch. But it also explained the novelist's careful distortion of facts, so that Dickens could draw the character of Nancy without mentioning the essential fact that she was a prostitute, and

Charlotte Brontë could draw a bedroom scene without a bed.

While the Gothic taste was drawing a veil of prettiness over Reality, Commerce was still busier making England ugly; thus combining Grace with Good Works. An unconscious revolution was taking place, and bewildered politicians fell back upon improvisations supported by moral attitudes, the method by which this country is habitually saved in a crisis. It was in this spirit that the Corn Laws were abolished because the potato was rotten in Ireland. It was in this spirit that John Bright opposed on moral grounds, the reduction of working hours for women and children in factories, holding that greater leisure for the working classes only meant more time for Vice; one more hour of leisure would be insufficient for adequate religious instruction but ample for Satan.

That it might also mean diminished profits for himself as a mill-owner was a thought which certainly never passed beyond the threshold of his unconscious mind.

When women were paid fivepence a day for binding Bibles it was solely that the Bible might be sold cheap so that it could reach the really poor (earning perhaps only fivepence a day).

It was the same spirit which permitted the great philanthropist, Lord Shaftesbury, to sympathise with sufferers in this world while gloating over the tortures of the damned in the next.

Or, to descend from great people to small, it was the spirit which made a young lady shudder at a mouse but relish a death-bed.

Was it not, simply, an excessive and disorderly flood of feeling which intoxicated the nation? Lacking scientific control it was a force let loose to sweep away whatever stood in its path, for it is characteristic that all the social reforms of the 19th century were effected when the nation was in a state of moral elevation; a mood originating in an awakening perception to suffering in others, followed by an intense desire to remove whatever distresses our own feelings; so that presently we regard this sympathetic discomfort as a proof of our moral superiority. From effecting a reform we derive a personal gratification surpassing that felt even by its beneficiaries.

Such was the emotional mood prevailing in the '40's; uncontrollable benevolence was the popular form of self-indulgence, restrained, in thoughtful people, by a fear that benevolence towards the lower orders might breed familiarity.

Oliver might learn to ask for more.

Indeed, just as rotten potatoes put Peel in his damned fright, so rotten social conditions aroused alarm in the minds of the prosperous. If once the Poor were to demand rights in the place of asking for charity anything might happen. The view is concisely expressed in a magazine for ladies, in 1843:

"The system of *levelling* which is now so much the rage must in the end overturn the whole state of society. Everything may be carried to excess which in the present moment is the case, in that extreme refinement of feeling which will ultimately be the ruin of England. Because the children and labourers in coal-mines endure many hardships (of their own choosing, as they are not slaves compelled to that employment) does that render it a crime for a nobleman who owns a colliery to give a fancy-ball? The over-refinement of our age discovers miseries of which our forefathers, who were far happier, never dreamed."

Hysterical reforms, poured out in a welter of emotion, are apt to engender moral attitudes in the reformers, and in this condition the nation, bubbling with emotion, stumbled headlong into the "Workshop of the World."

The Sentimental '40s

A fortunate section found themselves becoming rapidly rich; its women-folk, without preparation, were lifted into a higher social plane and demanded recognition of the fact. A new grade of society was invented for their benefit, and the word "Lady" took on a fresh and peculiar significance. As early as 1840 a book of Etiquette discusses the difference between a "Gentlewoman" and a "Lady," and explains that the former was born so, and the latter becomes so. A few years later, in 1846, an observer remarks: "Two of the most prominent signs of the time of moral advancement are increased sympathy and the importance attached to the cultivation of the female mind, in the last ten years. It is within a dozen years that a third class of gentlewoman has arisen, differing from the merely domesticated and the showy superficial misses. It is the moral qualities that have developed." . . . Qualities, or perhaps, Attitudes?

No one has ever succeeded in defining precisely the meaning of the word "Lady," as used in the Victorian sense. Certainly she was not necessarily an aristocrat, nor a plutocrat; merely to belong to the leisured classes did not suffice to give her the title. She recognised a gulf (for which she thanked God) between her and people in trade; this it was her care never to lessen, but she did not deny the gap between her and the Aristocracy; yet she claimed certain affinities with the latter and none with the former. Perhaps her forebears had come, not from the "Country" but from the "County," and instinctively she was aware that her peculiar mental outlook was similar to, if not identical with, that of the Best People.

Essentially she perceived life from a moral angle all her own, and it was her peculiar function to express by a moral attitude a justification of civilisation. It was not her task to *do*—that was the worker's: nor to *be*—that was the patrician's: but simply to feel; and the test of the Lady was the perfection of her feelings.

We can trace her beginnings from the period now under consideration, for she differed fundamentally from the "Lady" of the preceding decade; in the '30s it had been possible for a Lady to be coarse of speech and vulgar in manner, and even loose in conduct, but from the '40s onward an acute sensitiveness to the slightest deflection from the authorised version, marked the Lady, and maintained the standard. Henceforth she cultivated an evasive reticence of speech and thought, while manners became a ritual.

It is significant that from this period an abundance of little manuals of Etiquette poured forth to instruct the novice in the gentle art of becoming a Lady.

Her origin can be traced to the growing importance of the upper commercial and professional classes, whose women separated themselves from the stratum in which, it must be confessed, their roots had, often, been nourished, and now formed a new and important layer of their own, with their own code of manners, the slightest ignorance of which betrayed the horrid fact that you were "not quite."

But the distinction was much finer than merely conduct; it implied a mental attitude as well, and it took a generation to develop the full richness of its quality; however, in the '40s, the Lady was preoccupied with the task of inventing the rules and mysteries of the game; it had not yet become second nature.

The mental attitude was her fundamental distinction; she trained herself to view life, not in the romantic spirit as an adventure with Fate, but as an illustration of moral precepts. Life, and still more Death, was perpetually proving the truth of those rigid principles. She detected in every event a purpose, and her own function in the community was clear; she was to present a living picture of right-mindedness, illustrating to the rest the highest attainable refinement of thought and feeling. Contact with the outer world might impair her purity, and instead of experience she had Principles which could answer any question that Life might propound. She stood passively in a bustling world as a monument to the abstract virtues.

It was an inspired pose, coming at a moment when it could by its example raise the standard of the rest. Her feelings were easily touched, but the actual rectification of social wrongs was Man's work; for her it was enough to indicate them by sympathy. In that sense she became a powerful agent in reforming abuses without raising a hand.

But in spite of her rich fund of feeling there were aspects of her private life in which it was meet that the emotions should be stifled. It was her duty, as a wife, to love her husband, but it was her duty, as a lady, to do so without passion. So successful was she, indeed, that contemporary medical works state that the existence of such feelings, in a woman, were to be regarded as abnormal. Her mind shunned glancing at the coarser aspects of life; it was enough that the weaknesses of the flesh were confined to the male sex. The Curse of Eve, terrible though it might be, was not quite so shocking as the Curse of Adam. The correct attitude of the married woman was concisely put, in a work, *The Wives of England, their relative Duties, Domestic Influence, and Social Obligations* (1843): "I have spoken of the married state as one of the trial of Principle rather than the fruition of Hope."

One perceives that in becoming a Lady she had sacrificed her sense of proportion and therefore her sense of humour, so that by the coarse incongruities of life she "was not amused." But of innocuous fun she had a child's store; she could relish her husband's puns which helped a stiff party to thaw, and simple practical jokes, of a refined nature, were, of course, so very amusing. And when, of an evening, he would read aloud Mr. Dickens's last novel, how she would enjoy it all (except, perhaps, those bits that were almost too vulgar). In graver moments she would sigh for the suffering poor—indeed the ways of Providence were inscrutable!—and she wept copiously at the death of Paul Dombey.

Her attitude towards her husband, whom perhaps she would still address as "Mr.," was one of uncomfortable awe; he knew—oh!—everything; he owned everything (including herself and her belongings, for she could legally possess nothing); he was all-powerful, at least in the home. Of his business and his income she knew nothing. He regulated her life absolutely: read all her letters first, dictated her movements, chose her friends, ordered her pleasures. True he was a complete protection to her; behind that sure shield she was safe from anxieties, problems, doubts; a sort of Headmaster, wise, genial, or ferocious, under whose influence she never left school, or at least never entirely grew up.

But it was impossible to live even with a Headmaster, all those years without perceiving flaws in his perfection, to which it was her duty hastily to shut her eyes; weaknesses to be humoured, even, sometimes faults to be concealed from the family, for the secrets of the alcove must never be betrayed.

She might charm him, or coax him, or vex him, but she could never employ reason; it was not in the bond. She found herself never entirely natural in his presence, never wholly frank, for she never wholly knew him; and it dawned upon her that perhaps he never wholly knew her.

But in their common tasks of rearing the children, improving their social position, demonstrating their increasing refinement, the two worked wholeheartedly together. It was an "ad hoc" Alliance.

The young woman of that time was more happily placed; small emotional thrills supplied her wants; an air of kittenish incapacity played havoc on her adorers, and indeed towards the gentlemen she was always demurely playful, inspiring them with an etherealised emotion. It was ordained that this being from another world should, when ordered, stoop to conquer, and if possible, raise her conqueror. Until that happy moment arrived she viewed them all as possible beaux, and the furthest limit of her outlook ended in a halo of orange-blossom. Her life was mainly domestic. She regarded her mother with awe and her father with fear; the one inspired her with pity and the other with meekness. There was ample in the home to occupy her time, so that she had few temptations to indulge in thought, but she was no longer called upon to perform menial duties; if her parents were comfortably off, their daughters were young ladies who practised a thousand accomplishments and irrelevant refinements.

But there was a deadly temptation against which she must ever guard: a sin perpetually discussed in the magazines for ladies, and at social meetings, indeed wherever two or three were gathered together. It had suddenly sprung into being with the new code of conduct, the sin of "flirting."

Unfortunately the offence was not, at the time, defined, but it appears to have been a misdemeanour akin to playing with fire; on the highest moral grounds this was improper, lest a conflagration should arise, while from baser motives it was injudicious; a waste of matches. As she was destined for marriage a young lady must do nothing that might lower her prospects, and even—a terrible thought—leave her an old maid on her parents' hands.

A sin almost as deadly came into being about this time: to be or to seem "vulgar." Again it is unfortunate that, for the benefit of posterity, the term as used then was not clearly defined. We are told that they regarded the '30s as terribly vulgar, when ladies laughed aloud and showed their ankles; when chicken bones were gnawed in the hand, and girls were teased publicly about their beaux. Even in the '40s there were jolly old sherry-drinking aunts who *would* make such *common* jokes at Christmas about the mistletoe, and "hearts and darts, Misses and kisses"; it was so dreadful to say such things out loud, when they could be implied, with greater refinement, in a Valentine.

A contemporary woman writer describes the Young Ladies of her time, 1843:

"They wear their hair in two long ringlets hanging half out of curl, and a small flat curl fastened in a most miraculous fashion on either cheek. At parties whole bands of them sit together attired in white muslin with spotless kid gloves and exquisite bouquets. If addressed, the Young Lady replies in monosyllables with great demureness, languidly agreeing with her partner that it is almost too hot to dance, and seems relieved when at the conclusion of the set she can seek Mamma; at supper she takes nothing but a water-ice or the smallest of ratafia cakes. Mark the little start or scream which accompanies the explosion of crackers; and the bashfulness with which she positively refuses to show her motto. These young ladies are great novel readers, absolutely dote on Bulwer, think Mrs. Trollope very clever, only sometimes a little coarse. Byron they pronounce inimitable, and keep a duodecimo edition in their workboxes. They enjoy a play providing it is not too affecting, which makes one look such a fright afterwards; and can sit through an Italian Opera (without understanding a word) but are a little shocked at the ballet.

"The Young Lady is the most innocent being in existence, and will put on a look of the prettiest bewilderment when anyone ventures to converse with her on any subject beyond the usual routine. A young lady, asked whether she was a Whig or a Tory, replied she did not know but supposed she was the same as Papa.

"She does a great deal of needlework, such as embroidery on velvet, working slippers and bead purses and card-racks and pen-wipers, but is never guilty of mending her own stockings.

"At watering-places she always wears dust-coloured shoes and purple veil, and carries a parasol to save her complexion. In the country she usually dresses in white and carefully avoids walking on the grass in case it should be in the slightest degree damp. Then how she shrieks if a grasshopper skips across the path or a cow stops to gaze at her! When she comes to a stile what laughing and confusion and vowing to turn back for she is sure she can never manage to get over it—ending by doing so with the momentary display of a slender ankle.

"They never go into a passion, have no will of their own, never laugh out loud, or go anywhere without a gentleman, or take cheese at dinner—an odious vulgarism!"

Other sidelights on her mind—or the emotional attitudes which functioned as its substitute—can be derived from a study of the education to which she had been subjected. A contemporary, in 1847, urges that the Education of Women should have four cardinal features:

"1. The inculcation of moral and religious feelings. 2. Domestic duties. 3. General knowledge. 4. Accomplishments. Woman has been provided to soothe the more rugged Lords of Creation; like the tender vine which attaches itself to the rougher exterior of some other object so would she twine in gentleness and beauty around the stern image of the Universal Father."

Elsewhere the education of the upper-class young woman is described briefly as—"Languages, Music, Dancing, Painting and the light accomplishments; a sound religious education will supply most other deficiencies."

Such was the training which she received in her teens, supplemented by the reading matter supplied in the novels and magazines of that period. It is hardly necessary to add that much of this was educational, in the sense that it portrayed the correct attitude of mind which she was expected to adopt.

Thus, a story opens with this improving conversation:

"'Promise me that you will not grow weary, dearest, during the long years that must elapse ere I can claim the hand which now trembles in mine,' said Horace to her who had just plighted her troth to him.

"'You know me too well to believe so, Horace; I would fain see you content with your present prospects of success, and even at the risk of seeming most unmaidenly I will say that a mere competence with you would be all I should ask to ensure us happiness. Yet since you think the acquisition of wealth essential to your comfort it is not for me to oppose my wishes to your superior judgment.'"

Nothing could be more maidenly or in better taste.

On the other hand, the tale of "Sybil Lennard" is a dreadful warning—a story of the corruption of one who is a wife and alas! a mother, by "a depraved and Radical Member of Parliament, who sets to work to undermine her purity; Rousseau's works, Byron's poetry, and French Novels are the instruments of corruption." As the result of this unwholesome diet she abandons

"Looking towards my home and knowing I never more should call it mine." Drawn by E. Corbould as an illustration to *Family Secrets* or *Hints to those who would make Home Happy.* Published 1841

her home in the company of the depraved M.P.;
her husband dies of consumption and her
daughter becomes insane; truly a very radical
retribution. The reviewer of this novel remarks:
"This story is overwhelmingly affecting and
ought to be instructive; it shows how that an un-
worthy thought, unchecked, is often sufficient to
let in Satan" (thinly disguised as an M.P.). "Oh!
Woman! How careful should thy steps be when
one false movement may immerse thy life in a
deep pool of infamy! Thou art cared for by thy
God who has placed these gaunt terrors in thy
earthly career that He may claim thee pure and
undefiled, bright spirits for Beatitude and
Heaven!"

Elsewhere we are given a harsh picture of "a
young lady of uncertain years: that is to say, 28,
whose education has been superficial; showy
accomplishments took the place of a solid
foundation and the trash of a circulating library
filled her mind; thus she became 'romantic'; she
saw nothing but a spirit of chivalry pervading
everything."

But if such was apt to be her attitude of mind,
it must be pleaded in extenuation that it was
an almost necessary one, if she was to do her duty
and marry at 18 someone who would be, in sex,

person, and mind, a complete stranger. We cannot blame her for trying to gild the pill with sentiment.

That there were some who detected a flaw in this scheme of life may be deduced from an article, "The Grievances of Women":

"Picture an elegant, beautiful woman taking part in the vulgar squabbles of a vestry-room or entering the stormy arena of politics! Where then would be the quiet joys of domestic home? Our social condition would be changed and confusion and uproar would be triumphant. Woman's influence would be altered and her humanising influence destroyed. For women to attempt their social regeneration by agitation would be low and vulgar, independent of its being unfeminine. We are assured that the sensible portion of our fair countrywomen are content with the present social system and desire no change. The opposite sex love, respect and adore them and ever will, so long as they retain that inestimable jewel VIRTUE."

We shall hear the same lofty sentiments echoing down the ringing grooves of the Victorian era.

To marriage there was, of course, one terrible alternative; if through financial catastrophe a family was compelled to loose its clutch on the social ledge to which it had climbed a dreadful abyss opened below; the young lady fell headlong into the ranks of the Governesses of England. This new profession for women compared unfavourably with even the oldest; the degradation was similar if not so great; the work was harder and the pay worse; and by no stretch of imagination could it have been described as "a gay life."

The magazines of the '40s teem with descriptions, lamenting the facts but suggesting no substitute. "Why is woman considered to degrade herself by endeavouring to support herself?" asks one writer. "The Governess is a class rapidly on the increase; it is the only recourse left to young girls in the highest ranks of society who are forced to earn their living. At eighteen a governess professes to teach English in all its branches, French, German and Italian: singing, music and thorough-bass: painting in oils and water-colours: pencil and chalk drawing in every style: ornamental needlework, dancing and drilling. She may be known at a glance from her plain and quiet style of dress: a deep straw bonnet with green or brown veil; and on her face is a fixed sad look of despair."

We are not much surprised to learn that at this period governesses formed a larger proportion, than any other trade or profession, of the inmates of the asylums.

In the houses where she was employed she was treated with scornful patronage or veiled contempt. Had she not committed the unforgivable sin of falling from social grace? In a world of progress where every other family was busy scrambling up the scale, hers had slipped and fallen. But why this treading on her? Was it perhaps because a marriageable daughter was, in times of increasing wealth, something of an asset worth bartering, and the notion of an alternative career a thing to be discountenanced? For we find, later on when the upper classes are less prosperous, and superfluous daughters have become a liability instead of an asset, the reluctance disappears.

Whatever else a young lady had to learn, in the '40s, she had to acquire a nice familiarity with Etiquette, which is happily described as "The barrier which Society draws around itself, a shield against the intrusion of the impertinent, the improper and the vulgar."

We learn from one of these guide-books of the period (revised by a Lady of Rank) the details

that denote refinement; that at dinner the slices
of bread must never be less than 1½ inches thick.
"Than to offer thinner there can be nothing more
plebeian." On the other hand, table-napkins
("serviette" was a refinement yet to come) "are
by no means universally provided, and in their
absence a gentleman will use the tablecloth." It
had just become vulgar to eat pudding with a
spoon, or to imbibe soup from its tip. Such things
were vital.

The old word "genteel" was becoming vulgar
and even "lady," by constant over-use, "gentlewoman" being more select.

A proper knowledge of such matters was necessary for salvation; they had no meaning except
as shibboleths to expose the plebeian.

There were similar manuals of instruction in
"The Etiquette of Courtship and Marriage." The
former period, we are told—and can well believe
—"is one of agitating interest; a Lady should be
exceedingly cautious as to her manner of
receiving advances made by a gentleman, and
should, if they mature, at once refer him to her
Parents. She must never encourage the hopes of
one below her own station. When once engaged
it will be her duty to repress excess of ardour,
whether in her own case or in his, for nothing

is more likely to produce a diminution of respect. It is by no means desirable to appear in public with him too frequently, lest you excite remark, and attention from other gentlemen should be accepted with prudent reserve, for too great freedom may expose you to almost the worst reputation a lady can have, that of being a flirt.

"If she should break off her engagement her conduct will be unsparingly scrutinised and possibly condemned. . . . On her bridal day the pearls which decorate her brow are often contrasted with the drops which hang on her lashes, and the chastened pleasures of the occasion ought not to be represented by conspicuous pomp. The wedding tour is now usually taken by the happy pair without a companion."

It was at this point in her career that fiction was apt to end, for no novelist at that date envisaged further. But, it seems, that facts—perennial little facts—strewed her ensuing years. They helped to teach her the great lesson of resignation—so important for a woman to learn —for it seems that fifty per cent of the children would die before reaching the age of five.

An abundance of books on the Rearing of Infants was now beginning to appear on the market; their advice was admirable, and the consolation they offered (when the inevitable had happened) was uplifting.

The bride was not aware (one hopes) that the maternal mortality among the upper class was double that among countrywomen, who were deprived of the assistance of fashionable accoucheurs. It would not, of course, have been seemly for unmarried young ladies to be acquainted with such subjects.

In that period, to a woman the commonest phenomenon in life was death. As a girl it embellished the tales she read, and at an early age she became familiar with its details, sentimentally distorted, for it was customary for a corpse to hold a reception to which it invited all its relations. As she grew up the thing itself stalked at her elbow, for it must be admitted she herself was seldom in good health; the ravages of consumption were beyond record; in every family it had left a gap; some were decimated; friends, relatives, neighbours, were insidiously removed by its agency, and every young lady knew its symptoms and awaited their onset with a sort of peaceful expectancy, for it was, above all others, a most ladylike complaint. It supplied the pallid languor that denoted a refined mind; it became, indeed, almost a graceful accomplishment, and its minor features were studied and aped. In a little book, *The Girls' Book of Diversions,* she is taught "how to faint; the modes of fainting should be all as different as possible and may be made very diverting."

We may ascribe the tendency to fall into a decline either to the hand of Providence or to defective hygiene, according to whether we belong to that epoch or to this. It seems almost indelicate to pry into the pages of *The Handbook of the Toilet* (1841). It ascribes the British habit of "catching cold" (and all its grisly consequences) to draughts, the slightest exposure to cold, the imperfect closure of a door, or worse, a window. There are, of course, awful visitations beyond human control, doubtless dictated by Divine Wisdom and Benevolence, but we are assured that the British cold is not one of these; it is due simply to human carelessness. "For our fair countrywomen fear water; this, with insufficient clothing (a practice arising from the silly vanity of appearing small-waisted) are the true causes. A learned physician has recommended that the head should never be washed and the feet as seldom as possible, but such advice is absurd; a warm bath, all over, should be taken once a week, with perhaps a warm shower every morning, in which case shoes should be worn lest the feet are chilled in the process.

"The bed toilette should not be too ample. Many ladies who eschew flannel as a foe to small waists and therefore are too scantily clad by day, cover themselves with a profusion of clothing before they enter the bed (this being a feather mattress with curtains drawn). Ventilation of the room is desirable and for this purpose the grate should be kept open and even a small fire employed to create a draught." (For windows were securely shut against the dangerous night air.)

"Too many ladies rise in the morning with parched mouth and foul tongue, and without daring to wash the skin apply water to the face and hands only, or even dry-rub the face lest the complexion be spoiled."

As for the day clothing, the amount worn by a lady "at least over her vital organs is totally inadequate, and bare shoulders in evening dress is largely instrumental in starting consumption. The chest should be carefully guarded but the garments should be porous, and for that reason leather waistcoats and rabbit skins should be avoided. Flannel should be worn next the skin, all the year, over the whole body and arms and as low as the middle of the thighs; but alas! very few ladies will do so. Ladies should not be sparing of flannel petticoats, and drawers are of incalculable advantage to women, preventing many of the disorders and indispositions to which British females are subject. The drawers may be made of flannel, calico or cotton, and should reach as far down the leg as possible without their being seen."

The practice of tight-lacing is condemned, especially the use of stays lacing downwards, "producing injurious pressure upon those forms which Nature has given women as fountains of nourishment for their offspring; the downward pressure may even produce protrusion of the intestine, which has spoiled the prospects and fortune of many a girl who has brought it on herself."

The author supplies recipes for skin unguents, cosmetic washes, depilatories, rouge, pearl powder, teeth tinctures, hair dyes, Pomade divine (made of beef marrow) for the hair, washes, perfumes, and other necessaries of the toilet; for it appears that simple lavender bags are now vulgar, and more searching scents denote the lady.

But our author is scarcely fair in some of her strictures, for, in fact, most women were doing their best to preserve their health by wearing six petticoats, of which two were flannel. Nothing, however, would induce them to wear flannel next the skin, or to relax the tightness of their stays, in spite of repeated remonstrances from doctors and clergymen. "Tight lacing and sedentary languishing are the greatest enemies to female health," exclaimed the one. "Tight lacing, from a moral point of view, is opposed to all the laws of religion," protested the other, but even this reproof was ignored.

Some aspects of their lives can be deduced, by inference, from the advertisements appearing in the newly published *Lady's Newspaper* (1847 et seq). We are there made acquainted with "dress improvers," artificial busts, anti-consumption corsets, chest protectors, and specifics for pulmonary disorders; with "patent merino drawers, vests and union dresses, complete," and discover that those fascinating little side curls cost five shillings and sixpence. A dress could be made up for 5/-; a frilled nightdress cost 2/6d.; long-cloth chemise 1/2d.; ditto drawers 1/3d.; while "drawers, full·maids," are 8/6d. a doz. (but whether the maids are full of drawers, or the drawers are full of maids, is not clear).

Mourning garments are, of course, in constant

requirement, and are advertised, in most refined terms, as "Atramental and Lugubrious Attire."

This weekly newspaper for the fair sex reflects the feelings of its readers in sympathetic descriptions of public events, especially executions, and is fully alive to injustice to women. "Not a week passes without some glaring proof of the imperfect state of the Law for the protection of women." Of their rights it is less eloquent, but it appears that Women are not yet sufficiently guarded from the monster, Man, and further barriers are needed before the Lady can develop the virtues attainable only from splendid isolation.

There is a definite increase of interest in the welfare of children, and severe comments are made on the hardships inflicted on them in the form of punishment. A girl, aged 12, charged with having stolen from school a small prayer-book, is sentenced to fourteen days' hard labour, the magistrate regretting that he could not order a whipping as well: a sentence which the *Lady's Newspaper* regards as too harsh.

Women, with their abundance of sentiment, were now beginning to change their attitude towards children; these were no longer regarded as a kind of wild animal, but as a sort of human being, still steeped in sin it is true—their tainted origin necessitated that—but capable of salvation by copious doses of religion. The transformation from little devils into little angels was a painful process, but they could be trained into adopting moral attitudes; instead of physical pain, a more humane weapon was found to be spiritual fear. So they were taught to dread the insidious appeal of Satan, and still more, the terrible wrath of the Almighty, who, in His Infinite Goodness had prepared an Everlasting Fire of Brimstone for wicked little children who did not obey their dear parents. The method was proving much more effective than constant whipping, which indeed jarred upon the sensitive feelings of the '40s Mamma; so she invented a Deity to act as her deputy. It was a sentimental, sadistic age.

The price paid for refinement seems, on the whole, to have been somewhat heavy; cheerfulness and naturalness had to give place to affectation, and the new-born Lady found herself shut in with her superfluous emotions which she could not put to practical use; they swamped her surroundings and she trembled on the edge of hysteria: saved, perhaps, by abundance of domestic duties. They also induced a habit of mental sadism; death and disease supplied an agreeable refreshment to an otherwise dull married life, in which she was cribb'd, cabin'd and (frequently) confin'd. And when the end came, for she was likely to die under, rather than over the age of sixty, she was convinced she was going to a Heavenly Rest . . . and no doubt it was, heavenly.

But all the time she was supplying her generation with an uplifting Ideal; on such stepping-stones have we risen.

She played a part and looked it, for Woman's dress in the '40s had an air of a drawing-room ornament; comfort and convenience were minor points; the major effect aimed at was to present a demure prettiness, restrained by moral rectitude. The waist was as long as pointed stays could make it, and slanting revers from the shoulders sloped downwards and inwards to produce an inverted Gothic arch.

The bodice was moulded to the shape (or perhaps the shape was moulded to the bodice by aid of corset and concealed pads). The sleeves quickly lost the frivolous puffing at the elbows and became close fitting to the wrist; nothing could be more restrained. After the middle of the decade, however, an air of well-bred helplessness was affected by a sleeve expanding, bell-shaped, at the wrist, containing an exquisitely worked snowy under-sleeve, out of which peeped a hand looking, by contrast, extraordinarily small. No one could associate so fragile an ornament with toil.

The sleeve opening grew larger and larger, and the hand, consequently, smaller and smaller, as the owner became more and more ladylike and helpless. Meanwhile the skirt ensured a solid anchorage against any light airs, for it expanded into a ponderous dome of material, supported by bustle, horse-hair petticoat, two flannel petticoats, two plain petticoats, and a cambric one, wonderfully embroidered at the edge.

The length of the skirt concealed all but the toe so that walking was reduced to a graceful movement.

Over the upper half of the dress draughts were guarded against by some form of jacket, while out of doors a mantle, short behind and long in front, protected the fair wearer against the treacheries of the climate. Especial attention was devoted to the correct manipulation of the immense shawl; it could be applied with becoming grace if you were a lady, or with dreadful gaucherie if you were not quite.

It took time and privacy to arrange, and the

visitor, paying a call at the correct hours of 12 to 3, must not be invited to remove it.

The bonnet was the keynote of the age, a perfect symbol of meekness and modesty. The projecting wings shielded the blushing wearer from impertinent glances, while a peep in that direction was checked—it was hoped effectively, so that a view of the straight but narrow way was all that was permitted.

It must be confessed that in her ball-dress the young lady of the '40s seemed to have shed a good deal of that obscurity which by day rendered her so tantalising a speculation. For now neck and shoulders stood out like a champagne bottle from an ice-bucket. As she waltzed round the room her partner might well wonder, a little breathlessly, why the whole scaffolding did not collapse.

And, indeed, it was no simple matter, for young ladies cultivated such a shrug of the shoulder to keep the dress from slipping, that they developed spinal curvature; or at least the doctors of the day said so. But, if the secret must be betrayed, the dress stayed up simply by its tightness; underneath the Bertha every seam was straining, and the arms were held in a grip which made free movement of them impossible; for it was a peculiar feature of the dresses of that period for the bodice to be cut to embrace in it the upper portion of the shoulder. It was therefore impossible to raise the arm, or, in fact, to move quickly, to stoop, or recline with comfort. Such dresses were admirably designed for sedate company manners. And the materials used harmonised with such an existence; those delicate satins and taffetas for afternoon wear suggest attitudes of expecting aristocratic Sunday visitors.

The voluminous white muslins, the four, five or six flounces, scalloped and embroidered—for the number of flounces increased annually during the decade—and the acreage of white petticoats, stiff and starched, conjure visions of pure maidenhood, and a huge washing day to follow. Alas! to be a Lady was becoming an expensive luxury.

The fashion for soft colours, especially for secondary and tertiary tints, indicated growing refinement; for those dreadful '30s were now seen to have been excessively vulgar. In the '40s they favoured colours that were bright without brilliance, and to suit the heaviness of the skirt, broad effects were obtained in the form of monochromes of yellow, blue, or pink, softened by decorative effects of lace or ribbon. Any suggestion of boldness was carefully eschewed, and wherever possible lines met in Gothic angles. It imparted a faint but pleasant suggestion of a stained glass window, luminous but not transparent, concealing the contents from Man's understanding.

To such the Man of the day succumbed, for he found that Woman is never so attractive as when she is incomprehensible.

Chapter VI

The Perfect Lady of the '50s

TOWARDS the end of the '40s a wave of
Liberalism had arisen in Europe, washing
away ancient ideas of government, religion, and
the relationship of class to class; on the Continent street barricades resumed their functions
against whizzing bullets, and monarchs scuttled
for the frontiers. Meanwhile the flood, in a
modified form, poured over England, nourishing
a crop of moral reforms.

All through the '50s there was an increasing
consciousness of the moral obligations due from
us to our fellow-beings. It became the duty of
the fortunate to help the unfortunate, not merely
by sympathy but by practical aid; a motion not
entirely inspired by religion, although that
impulse was growing in strength, but also by a
new sense of citizenship. It was becoming an
obligation of the modern state. But the conception that perhaps the unfortunate owed their condition to the fortunate, was, as yet, not enter-

tained, and the notion that citizenship implied equality of rights was beyond the imagination of all except a small band of philosophic Radicals.

It was an age when Charity was regarded as the only practical cure. Besides, to be charitable is more virtuous than to be taxed, and costs less. For behind this wave of Liberalism there were visions of another, a more grimy flood, bringing with it horrid threats of Democracy. Thoughtful observers perceived that it would be wise to direct the first into orderly channels to diminish the shock of the second. They apprehended the possibility of "an ugly rush," and charity redoubled its efforts. Fortunately the English mind is incapable of feeling fear; that crude emotion, detectable in so many other nations, becomes, in our own psychology, sublimated on to a higher plane. The spectacle of injustice arouses our moral indignation and we hasten to rectify it, thereby escaping a danger without loss of pride. Indeed, the national conscience glows with increased satisfaction and security.

It was in such a mood that England handled the problems which faced her in the '50s. The disintegrating force which had wrecked the Continent assuaged and nourished the moral elements of the British people. Its effect upon the women of England was particularly great, and in that one decade they developed more, perhaps, than in any other, before or since. The "Lady," that new social class which had recently come into existence, suddenly emerged from her narrow domesticity, and stepped into the light. Mere sentiment, which had hitherto satisfied her emotional life, was now found insufficient; she demanded some more active mode of expression. Emotions are intended as a prelude to action, and the wealth of sentiment cultivated in the preceding years now stirred the Lady to discover fields wherein to display her powers. But her powers were, as yet, emotional rather than intellectual; as she surveyed the world to which her eyes were now opening she felt its harsh incongruities without understanding them. "The tendency of her education being to add greatly to the variety of her mental resources" (remarked a woman writer in 1851), "Woman's danger is more from the head than the heart; she is looking for a field of activity for the mind and is suffering from an excess of wonder." In a word, she was wanting to use her mind before it was trained. She had the attitude of one stepping out of a dungeon into the light of day; under such conditions perception is over-sensitive but discrimination confused.

If we examine the numerous magazines for women, of this period, we shall obtain from them probably more reliable information as to feminine mentality than from the writings of more eminent but masculine philosophers. It is from such sources that the quotations given in this chapter are mainly derived.

Thus, in 1855, comment is made on "the want of harmony that pervades the age; the restless anxious desire to embody thought in actual life; the dissatisfaction that the actual falls short of the ideal, and the want of faith in truth."

The magazines themselves have expanded in outlook and seriousness; they assume, on the part of their readers, a capacity to grasp problems and to form opinions, which is a new and significant feature. Some are becoming educational, some cling to the safe soporifics, but they are losing the old sweet nursery tone, and all are impressively moral. From such a source it is the more striking to find, as the decade opens, the frank statement of woman's views. "We must confess we feel no great veneration for our ancestors. The great struggle of the age is to escape from the bondage of the past. The present is an age of surprises . . . the mystical emotion

138

and subjective ideality which have only sprung into being in recent years . . ." Such phrases, even if the terms are a little vague, convey a notion which would have found no place in the women's magazines of ten years earlier. The sense of surprise is reiterated; whatever the average man may have thought of the period through which he was passing, it seems that the average woman regarded it as something startling. But then the man had not come into it out of a dungeon.

The matter in the magazines indicates that Woman was beginning to look beyond the confines of her own life. She directed her attention to the condition of the Poor, as a suitable object on which to expend her wealth of feeling; she became aware that there were fifty thousand women, in this country, working for less than sixpence a day, and from the newspapers (at which she was beginning to peep when her husband permitted the favour), she discovered that in 1851 some 336,000 people escaped from an intolerable poverty by emigration.

But she was no longer satisfied to expend sympathy; she began to go forth and look at these queer results of masculine statesmanship; and visiting the homes of the Poor became a fashionable habit for women of leisure. Of the effect on the Poor we have no evidence, but certainly the practice was beneficial to the lady of leisure. Her mind, wholly without scientific training, was naturally unable to distinguish between cause and effect, and the things seen were so shocking to her feelings that all she aspired to do was to remove the more obvious features. In this spirit she carried, on her visits to the hovels of the Poor, inspiring little books. It was disappointing to find that Vice and Starvation were not immediately cured by Religion and Beef-tea, although both were made of the best British materials.

With similar enthusiasm she urged the Lower Orders to abandon that degrading habit of taking intoxicating liquor to excess, for while the Better Classes had by now greatly improved in this respect, the Lower seemed disinclined to make any effort in that direction. It was impossible, we read, at that date for a lady, though accompanied by a gentleman, to walk down Tottenham Court Road in the evening, on account of the number of drunken people lying in the gutter. The Temperance Movement received her cordial approval, at least, as regards its spread among the People (for Ladies required support when—

as was so often the case—they were in delicate health). Its encouragement was not lost sight of in the magazines. Thus, in 1854, a reviewer remarks: "The Band of Hope Almanack would make no bad ornament above a poor man's hearth, and while informing him, might help to reform the besetting sins of poverty, intemperance and uncleanness. Some of our lady readers, in visiting the houses of the labouring classes, would find it a very useful little gift."

And, although it might have been inadequate as a substitute for soap, how the hungry Labouring Classes must have devoured its pages, especially its poetic panegyric:

> "Water, sparkling water,
> Earth's primeval daughter,
> O'er the world prevail;
> Gift from Heaven descending,
> Adam's race befriending,
> Hail! For ever hail!"

In the opinion of the reviewer, "When the children of the poor are taught such rhymes as these, Virtue may yet hope to escape the mud-oceans of pollution and misery which are about to overwhelm our social system. . . ." Such are the powers of hail, for ever hail.

The Lady's impulse to seek out suitable recipients on whom to pour her superfluous emotions, tinged always with a flavour of moral superiority, inspired her with an enthusiasm for nursing the sick. There is something not altogether disagreeable in witnessing the misfortunes of others, especially, when, as is so often the case, they can be traced to moral delinquences. It all seems such a clear proof of Divine intention, while the more fortunate visitor is evidently in special favour. The peculiar gratification which the Victorian lady, from the highest to the lowest, derived from the spectacle of a sick-bed—or, better, a death-bed— may be traced to a consciousness of not merely physical but moral superiority over the weaker brethren. Of course, the cynic, always so ready to detect the basest of motives, might attribute this taste to sadism, through which the spectacle of suffering, in itself, affords pleasure irrespective of the personality of the victim. But the Victorian Lady at that period displayed no morbid interest in the sufferings of lower animals, for example, but only in those human beings near enough to herself to remind her of her own advantages. The charge of sadism, therefore, is unjust.

Death supplied the perfect moral picture; the contrast, heightened by every artifice of crape and trappings, between herself and the thing lying there, was a clear demonstration of Divine selection. It seems, therefore, the Victorian interest in sick-nursing arose from the Victorian sense of personal well-being.

Already in 1850 an "Institution for training Nurses" was started in Fitzroy Square, where, it appears, as many as four ladies were bold enough to face the training, during the first year. It required the impetus derived from the picturesque figure of Florence Nightingale, as sketched by war-correspondents, before the movement became really attractive. It is to our credit that none of our wars have been entirely without some resulting benefit; the Crimean War certainly created Sick Nursing as a new outlet for feminine energy.

A profession came into being on a flood of sentiment (in honour of a woman who hated sentiment, and who established a tradition that it must never be displayed in nursing). It seemed to afford a suitable career for the fastidious, fluttering English Lady in whose hands a hasty improvisation has somehow become the only profession for women which is not subjected to hostile criticism.

Even in the '50s the effect of this discovery was considerable. It became impossible to regard any longer the purely domestic as woman's only suitable sphere. As a sick nurse she appeared to be more successful than as a mother, and the notion arose that possibly she might do equally well in other directions. Bold spirits aimed at Medicine, but as a magazine of 1859 sagely observed, "It is impossible that a woman whose hands reek with gore can be possessed of the same nature or feelings as the generality of women"; and the figure of Dr. Elizabeth Blackwell was regarded with well-bred horror.

Meanwhile the desire grew apace to rectify the habits, especially the moral habits, of those incapable of defending themselves from such improvements. Ladies discovered in their own homes an ample supply in the shape of domestic servants, whose manners and morals required urgent attention. It was one of those happy moments when servants were cheap and abundant; in 1850 London alone contained ten thousand female servants always out of a place. The Lady's attitude towards them is admirably expressed in a magazine of 1853. "There is no doubt that servants as a class are exceedingly ill-prepared for the offices of responsibility they are required to hold. If they are fitted by their skill to take part in the coarser machinery of our homes they want the judgment and high tone of morale to work in unison with its finer directing impulses."

It was the obvious duty of the mistress to superintend the spiritual education of her domestics, to penetrate into their personal affairs and rectify them according to her own views, to curb inclinations to philandering, to check extravagance (on a wage of £12 a year) and instil proper respect for their betters.

In spite of these efforts the results seem to have been unsatisfactory, but the blame must be traced to extraneous sources, for we are told, in 1859, that "one of the great causes of the poor type of servant is the very superfluous education given in our national schools, leading many of the girls into sinful and criminal courses."

It was deplorable that the Lower Orders would not remain quiet in that station in life in which it had pleased the Victorian God to place them. It almost seemed that religion was wasted on them. However that may have been, the new spirit of enterprise was reaching young women of the lower middle class, and in 1854 women clerks, suitably chaperoned, were employed in the Electric Telegraph Company in Manchester, an innovation which the Ladies, from their superior position, viewed with approval. The work was beneficial to society and, apparently, perfectly moral. They further urged that men shop-assistants should be replaced by women, at least in drapery departments, for there was a feeling of indelicacy in buying stockings from a man.

In fact, in every direction an air of refinement was blowing away the coarse habits of the past. Its purpose, as directed by the Ladies of England, was to temper the violence of that reforming spirit which seemed to possess the man of affairs, and with feminine tact persuade it to remove impurities rather than inequalities of the landscape.

The ladylike aim was to make the social fabric sweeter without disturbing its essential configuration, but it seems that in the process of blowing away decayed matter it is difficult to preserve the picturesque. Towards the end of the '50s, complaints creep into the ladies' magazines that perhaps the display of energy has been misdirected. "Within the last ten years or so you have had agitation enough to surprise the most phlegmatic; Ireland, America's slave-trade, Jews' Bill, Temperance, Early Closing Movement, National Education, Spiritualism, Crimean War, Bloomerism. . . . It is not Reform these people want but change. The branches and not the roots have been struck. To every discontented Woman's-Rightist it may be said that the real source of grievance lies in yourself. There is not an occupation a woman ought to think of which is not at present open to her. The professions and public offices are, very properly, closed to her; but women can teach, keep shop, write books, do needlework, draw, play. . . . It is high time, if any good is ever to be effected, that the Women of England ceased talking and commenced working. But in most cases it is Woman's mission to save—rather than to make—money."

The old problem of the Governess still provoked discussion. In a material sense her position had improved; her salary had risen from £30 or £40 per annum to £50 or £60, but the social stigma remained, so that if a daughter of gentlefolk adopted that career she must expect to be regarded as one who had lost caste. This entailed many disadvantages; a correspondent, in 1851, is informed: "Your own good sense will show you that honourable attachment is rarely formed for a governess by a gentleman."

Nevertheless, the recent publication of *Jane Eyre* had raised the drooping spirits of countless governesses throughout the land, who were agog to throw themselves into the arms of Mr. Rochester as soon as he turned up. The notion was a disquieting one to their employers, and mothers concealed the book from daughters displaying any symptoms of the Rochester complex.

A young lady in 1850 asks, "Is it bad taste and coarseness to admire *Jane Eyre?* Is it an improper book?" Well, it was certainly a disturbing one, and it was the principle of the Lady to suppress such things in her personal sphere. All through this period her policy was Amelioration without Upheaval.

In another direction *Jane Eyre* had done more serious mischief; innumerable young ladies set to work to produce variations of it, without, however, being Charlotte Bröntes. The tale is, after all, but a version of the Cinderella legend with which every romantic girl tells herself to sleep; masses of these now reached publication and served, at least, to show that women could write fluently.

In her search for appropriate subjects

MEETING OF THE "BLOOMER" COMMITTEE. The *Lady's Newspaper*, 1851

deserving Amelioration without Upheaval the Lady cast her eye on unfamiliar places. Her visits to the cottage and the slum brought to her attention problems of health and sanitation. She could no longer regard disease as an act of God, to interfere with which would be impious, for epidemics of cholera and diphtheria were rife in the '50s and had a horrid way of spreading from the slum to respectable quarters, so that it seemed clear that they must be in some way connected with bad sanitation, for even in the best houses it must be confessed that drainage was poor. In 1851 Parliament itself, in its enthusiasm for bad smells, detected that all was not well in Palace Yard; a Commission was appointed and the Minister was able to inform an attentive House that "the Commissioners are at present sitting on three cesspools which are considered necessary to remove the evil"—a picturesque instance of Amelioration without Upheaval. Up and down the country Ladies imitated, in a less sedentary fashion, the example, and implored the Poor to practise cleanliness.

The condition of Children also came under their survey, and in the same year Day Nurseries were started, from which the Ladies, coming as benevolent visitors, derived some useful instruction, so that, in 1853, it was possible for a magazine to state: "For some years past the old-fashioned method of bringing up children, the extreme reign of terror, has passed away." We are not so concerned with the effect of this change upon the children as upon the mothers. The fatalistic attitude gave way to one of enquiry; the old method of training children through Terror to Triumph was softened, and that some thought was now being devoted to the subject is evidenced by the increasing number of domestic guide-books.

In effect the change was in the direction of persuasion, playing upon the feelings of the child, stimulating them by religious exhortations on the one hand and appeals to social caste on the other. To be good was not enough, but to behave like a little gentleman was even better.

It would be harsh to describe this as a process of turning children into snobs and prigs, for as the offspring of their parents they were that already; besides it is easy to underrate the advantages derived from such attitudes; they were not merely the product but in a measure the cause of the growing superiority of the Nation. It was getting rich with fatal facility so that it was impossible for the comfortable classes not to feel extraordinary exhilaration. It was their firm conviction that British ideas, British customs, British goods and British religion were immeasurably the best in the world, and that it was our moral duty to export them to less fortunate nations. In a burst of frankness the *Lady's Newspaper* of 1850 exclaims: "It is certainly a pleasant thing to think well of oneself; unhappily this is our national vice."

And yet it was recognised that absolute perfection had not been quite arrived at; in the domain of religious thought—so important to the feminine mind—much remained to be done. The plainer forms of Protestantism appeared, at least to the Lady, to lack charm, while being perfectly adapted to the requirements of the people. For her a more ladylike form of worship was needed and it seemed possible to borrow, without obligation, from Rome some of her ameliorating effects. Out of these materials an upper-class creed was presently evolved, leaving Dissent for the lower orders.

"Church" and "Chapel" became almost distinctions of class, for we are a practical nation and like our religions to match our rank in life. Religion was a fashionable topic in good society at this period. The High Church Movement on the one hand, and Papal Aggression on the other, filled columns of the papers while the Gorham Judgment was thrashed out in every respectable drawing-room. What it was all about is perhaps less important than the fact that Women began to discuss religion instead of accepting it blindly, an innovation which aroused some apprehension. "We would fain see her the Prop and not the Bellows in assisting to maintain the high sincerity of religious convictions," was the advice given to Ladies by one of their own magazines in 1850. On the other hand a mass of books and pamphlets were published to arouse women to greater activity. We read that "the literary world is in danger of being flooded by publications designed for the intellectual improvement of the female sex"; and in spite of their appearance we must suppose these books were read.

At the same time we detect in the novels of the period a subtle change of tone, and remembering that women have always been great readers of novels we must assume that the new tone was adapted to their change in taste.

"The day for the moral novel is past; the tone of our modern novel is not moralising"—

and yet within a few years of this criticism, *The Mill on the Floss* appeared. (But, then, there is moralising and moralising.) Gone, at least, was the treacly sentiment of the '40s with a moral borrowed from melodrama; in its place a more insidious form of self-esteem arose; a habit of detecting moral defects in others. It was the habitual attitude of the '50s.

Now that the Perfect Lady was claiming to establish a standard of correctitude towards which it was the duty of Man to struggle, and to which other nations turned envious eyes, it was natural she should consider the relative positions of the sexes to each other. The legal privileges of the husband had, till now, been great. "It is not lawful for a wife to live apart from her husband with a separate maintenance, unless his violence has put her in fear of her life; mere flogging is not enough," had been the dictum of the judges. It seemed hardly compatible with the new rôle Woman intended to play. The change was recognised reluctantly by the spiritual-minded, and in 1857 the Divorce Act was passed, to the pious horror of Mr. Gladstone; by it Woman obtained the privilege of physical decency.

Already, in America, the "Woman's Rights

Movement" had come into being, and uneasy ripples of it were crossing the Atlantic, wafting to these shores an extraordinary phenomenon, a woman wearing trousers. Mrs. Bloomer appeared, gave lectures, demonstrated the comforts of a curious costume, and vanished, leaving behind the memory of a name usefully attached to an indescribable garment.

The chief objection to the lady was not her clothes but her country; she seemed the herald of a dreadful democracy. The English Lady of the '50s was not prepared to accept her fashions from a plebeian people whom her ancestors had regarded as runaway servants. Besides she did not desire liberty of limb, but respect of person.

Long past were the days when Woman was content to receive Favours at Man's hand; she had now acquired what seemed to her more valuable than Rights, extraordinary Privileges. As a Lady she was excused from toil, from having to earn money, from payment of her debts, from a host of penalties which were shelved on to her husband, from soiling her mind with distasteful things; she was free from serious criticism because she had not to measure her abilities against Man's.

In a world of professionals she reigned as an

amateur, adopting with dexterity the appropriate attitude; patronising her inferiors, suave to her equals, and conscious that on a moral plane she had no superiors. She had won a privileged position in this world and the next. By the end of this decade the Perfect Lady had reached an altitude which appeared final for she stood at the apex of civilisation.

No wonder that the growing clamour for "Women's Rights" jarred upon her ear, for instinct warned her that the winning of Rights would probably entail the loss of Privileges. As it was, she had accomplished much in half a century and could survey her world with complete satisfaction.

There remained, however, the task—or rather the moral duty—of rendering her position impregnable, and planting her principles on her surroundings. A certain uneasiness was provoked when Radicals bellowed their grotesque doctrines. The shadow of Demos stretched in her direction and she experienced a shiver; her daughters, too, sometimes had odd ambitions. It was disturbing that they should be told, in 1857, in one of their own magazines: "In the present year of grace girls are educated for one solitary purpose in existence and that is to get husbands.

They will never be respected until girls are taught some higher aim in life than that of 'bagging husbands.' "

But what higher aim could a young lady have?

And some were cultivating manners that alarmed their Mammas. "It is now thought clever for young ladies to be loud, positive and rapid; to come into a room like a whirlwind; to express ideas of their own in language which, twenty years ago, would only have been understood in the stable." It seems, too, that "Affectation has long ceased to be the fashion," and in its place a new social sin was creeping in, for "one great discredit to the present day is the 'fast young lady.' She talks of 'the men,' and prefers sitting with them when they are smoking; she plays billiards and shows a marked antagonism to her own sex. She has a blasé look and a free tongue." This sort would even practise the sport of "bagging husbands" that had already been bagged. . . . The same authority states that difficulties were created by two other sorts of modern girl, namely the Prude, who refused to play the game when ordered, and the Blue Stocking who "thinks of nothing but Tennyson and Browning," and so misses chance after chance. No wonder Mammas agreed that "Demoralisation is rapidly increasing in all classes."

And yet, if she would only realise it, how simple is Woman's problem!

At the beginning of this disturbing decade it had been succinctly put in an article "How to manage a Husband": "Our first great secret is that a Woman should make herself necessary to her Husband; the next that she should convince him she cannot be happy without him. Perhaps there never was a period in which the influence of women was so little visible; it is almost wholly confined to domestic life. Husband and Wife agree to pass the rest of their lives together with no more knowledge of each other's tastes than has been gathered from the small talk of the evening parties."

Ten years later bewildered husbands were demanding how to manage a wife. But at the beginning of this period there still lingered the old attitude that men were deceivers ever—at least in the more homely sections of the community where tradition dies slowly. We must suppose it was for them that a work, *The Perfect Lady*, was designed, for it is truly eloquent in its warnings. "We caution our fair readers against the designs of treacherous men. How many lovely forms fade away into the tomb and none can guess the cause that blighted their loveliness! The charm of existence is at an end; dry sorrow drinks her blood and presently she sinks into her untimely grave, brought down to darkness and the worm."

The magazines teem, in fact, with good advice to Young Ladies to an extent that arouses suspicion. Perhaps it was necessary to remind them that "it is unusual for a young lady to walk alone with her affianced lover; that they should see each other only in the presence of a third person is, perhaps, an error on the right side. Man is encroaching and Woman is easily worked upon through her pity, gratitude or her love, to permit of those little familiar caresses which, experience shows, often extinguish the Man's love while increasing the Woman's. Long *tête-à-têtes* between lovers are certainly not likely to increase in Man that reverence which forms part of all true love."

And they are warned, in the plainest terms, that "if you marry without your parent's consent, remorse will haunt you till your dying hour."

The magazines devoted to the improvement of the rising generation began, once more, to advise anxious enquirers, and the replies given indicate a consistent policy. Thus, Phœbe, at sixteen, has already formed an attachment to a young man but is certain her parents would disapprove; "she feels that a sense of duty would enable her to conquer her own inclinations but she cannot endure the thought of her lover's misery." But, really, the solution is simple. She *must not* continue to receive his attentions.

"Neglected One" describes herself as "the only plain girl in a family of beauties; the mortifications she suffers are perfectly crushing." Again, the solution, like the young lady, is plain. "She should resolve to be amiable and accomplished and she will be loved yet."

For our better information we are given a precise list of such accomplishments. "Elegant Arts for Ladies comprise the making of Feather Flowers, Hair Ornaments, Flowers and Fruit in Wax, Shell Work, Porcupine Quill Work, Painting on Vellum, Velvet and Glass, Gilt Leather Work, the gilding of Plaster Casts, Bead and Bugle Work, Seaweed Pictures, and the mysteries of Diaphonie and Potichomanie."

An advanced curriculum, perhaps, but "every young lady should learn to dance, and nothing is more captivating than the power of singing sweetly; she should play the piano, and drawing is a quite elegant accomplishment, while French and German are now indispensable."

A regime, one perceives, offering small scope

for Satan to find mischief still. . . . The correct behaviour for Young Ladies is described in a multitude of articles so that they could be in no doubt as to the finer distinctions between the Well-bred and the less-well-bred; for alas! both sorts are now to be found among the Gentry, that is to say, "the learned and liberal professions and all engaged in mercantile and literary pursuits."

Good breeding consisted of strict attention to masses of minor irrelevances. Thus: "Young ladies may visit their acquaintances alone but never appear alone in public. In these modern and enlightened times a lady may walk un-attended in the street, provided she does not loiter or look round, but nothing would excuse the gross impropriety of her being out alone after dusk." It would be unseemly to shake a gentle-man's hand; her own must be offered passively and quickly withdrawn. Indeed her attitude to-wards the male sex must ever be guarded. "No lady should allow herself to believe in a man's attachment to herself until he has given her proofs that admit of no doubt of his devotion. Of all proofs of ill-breeding the greatest is setting down as proofs of love what are, perhaps, only the common attentions of a polite gentleman."

A conversation between a mother and her

engaged daughter, narrated in 1857, supplies further light on this important matter.

" 'I sometimes fear, Mamma, I am not as passionately in love as I ought to be. Do you think so, Mamma?'

" 'Quite, my love. A true woman's love is, in the first instance, mainly composed of gratitude and pity. Gratitude for his affection and pity for his loneliness.'

" 'I trust he will not be deterred by finding me the niece of the widow of a brewer who was only a respectable man pretty well off. . .'

" '. . . My love, your aunt in St. John's Wood is a true lady, though a brewer's widow. . . .'

" 'What is your opinion of Platonic love, my dear Mamma? . . .'

" 'Platonic love is rather the fashion to chat about just now among young ladies, but I don't think there is such a thing; or, at least, young ladies ought to have nothing to do with it. . . .'

" 'If I marry, dear Mamma, it must not be one who will rob you of a daughter but add the blessings of a son. . . .'

" 'That, my love, would be the wish of every Christian gentleman who married a good and dutiful daughter. . . .' "

It seems almost an anticlimax when this

enquiring young woman asks what is the ladylike method, at dinner, of removing cherry-stones from the mouth; but maternal advice is never at a loss. " 'Once in they must come out, my love; but I advise the well-bred lady to avoid such dishes.' "

If we may accept this as a common type at that period we must recognise that there were others, for already some divergence was beginning to appear between those holding Orthodox views, clinging to Privilege and Ritual as the correct attitudes for Ladies, and the Heretics with their revolutionary notions of Liberty, Equality and—one fears—Fraternity. It is always the Orthodox who govern the prevailing Fashions, for the "Orthodox" means merely the Majority, and "Morals" their habits.

In the early '50s the Gothic inspiration had reached its zenith, and the sharp angular effects, so noticeable in the costumes of the '40s, became now broadly massive. It was a period when "extravagance in dress is one of the prevailing vices of the age," and it extended rapidly down the social scale so that at the close of the decade it was said "in modern days the distinction in dress between the higher and the middle classes is in many respects nullified. Women of the middle class to meet the demands of finery which they consider themselves bound to have, are accustomed to forgo an additional servant, to cut down the cost of their children's education and even their household's food."

It was an age of display; "the present fashions permit of a profusion of ornament which a little while ago would have been considered vulgar." The growing dimensions of the skirt seemed to symbolise Woman's increasing place in the world; by 1856 a silk dress required 18 to 20 yards of material. The former methods of sustaining an edifice of such dimensions were now ineffectual; in 1854 we read: "The petticoats worn, especially in evening dress, are stiffer than ever; the hoops of our grandmothers cannot have been much wider than the skirts of a fashionable lady to-day." In the same year, "not satisfied with the Bustle, some ladies of the present day have revived the practice of wearing hoops." Thus was evolved the famous Artificial Crinoline, at first a hooped skeleton skirt, then a wired petticoat, and in 1857, the perfected article, the Watch-Spring Crinoline (costing from 15/- to 30/-). As the size of the skirt expanded, its shape altered, becoming less of a dome and more of a triangle; until at the end of the decade Woman

163

had evolved a new shape for herself; she resembled the Great Pyramid. No longer human, she appeared a cipher encaged in a symbol, expressing as it did, her dignity, solid attractions and aloofness from the Lower Orders. The Crinoline suggested a barrier against the elbows of encroaching Democracy, an attempt to sustain a social conception which was nevertheless fated to collapse.

The Gothic taste for angulation could be carried no further, for Woman had become one great Triangle; in a single generation she had changed from a Minx to a Monument. But even grandeur had its drawbacks, and the Crinoline *was* inconvenient. In a magazine of '58 a young correspondent, describing herself as "Peach-blossom" is advised not to attempt the climbing of stiles, in a crinoline, for the task is impossible; and if she suffers much from the comments of vulgar little boys it would be better, in a high wind, to remain indoors.

The Crinoline fashion was condemned as ruinously expensive. "Your lady's maid must now have her crinoline and it has even become essential to factory girls." We get some idea of its widespread use from the fact that in 1859 Sheffield was producing wire for half a million crinolines a week.

The fashion was also a dangerous one, for numbers of wearers were burnt to death from approaching too near a fire. The complaints of the men were bitter; with three or four of these gigantic ladies in an ordinary drawing-room, the men could not get beyond the door. Omnibus drivers discovered that their vehicles, designed to take "eight insides," would hold no more than four. Abuse, sermons, and ridicule were poured out in vain; Man was powerless against this new Colossus dominating his world. And Woman clung to her Crinoline, in spite of everything, because it demonstrated to the unbelievers her new significance.

In the upper half of her costume the Lady expressed the widening gap between her and those who performed manual labour. The sleeves expanded at the ends into caverns filled with white foam, out of which peeped fairy hands; velvet, the least practical material for a worker, was appropriate for the Lady of Leisure, who would wear silk of a morning as a proof that her wardrobe contained no second-best.

The toilet became an elaborate function. "In no particular has the present generation become more fastidious than in what is requisite in ladies' dressing-rooms."

The "fast young lady," with those masculine proclivities, borrowed notions from the men and appeared in waistcoats; to call them "gilets" was a poor defence; they were indelicate, bold and a sign of depravity. At the same time bonnets had shrunk away so that the face was frankly visible. Although the waist was still long and the bodice pointed, the stiffness of it had disappeared, for in fact tight lacing was going out of fashion. Stays without whalebones revealed the pattern Nature had originally drawn, and pretty figures once more disturbed Man's equanimity. Those inaccessible charms were indeed exasperating; for who, across an acre of crinoline, could come to grips with such a subject? But it was the aim of the Perfect Lady to be ever slightly out of Man's reach.

Chapter VII

The Revolting '60s

THE pure Gothic impulse, with its angular symbolism and its sentimental attitude of mind, was subsiding rapidly after the early '60s. A new phase in Woman's development began, and with it a new mode of symbolic form.

Before considering the new it may be convenient to glance back over the old. While there is always, perhaps, in the English people, an under-current of sympathy for Gothic Attitudes, the flood tide which arose in the '20s swept the country for some forty years; we have seen how it affected the relationship of the sexes; how it led to Woman's concealing herself from Man's view until she appeared to him as an incomprehensible equilateral triangle before which he was prepared to bow down and worship without attempting to understand the mind of his idol.

All during this Gothic epoch any suggestion of exhibitionism was steadily suppressed, and

Man grew accustomed to regard Women as the Great Unknown. With the rise of the Perfect Lady and the growing prosperity of her class, the principal means of sex-attraction was the dowry. The man was content to marry a stranger so long as the precise sum was attached to her person. And so long as prosperity permitted the dowry to be a comfortable one the method answered. A blank in the lottery was the act of God.

But when women began, during the '50s, to emerge from their seclusion and enter the world, they were no longer unknown quantities; and presently the prosperity of that class began to diminish. Cost of living during the '60s steadily increased (due partly to the growing demand for luxury, partly to the influx of Californian gold, and partly to the new and expensive tastes of women who were no longer content to economise at home); so that in '68 it was said that £1000 was not worth more than £600 had been, thirty years before.

As a result the old form of sex-attraction failed to answer.

Pathetic were the lamentations of parents, brought up in a sterner school, who traced the evil, as parents will, to "the guilty and growing

168

luxury of the age which prevents men from marrying early."

The young man was wont to reply that the modern girl might be amusing to flirt with but as a permanency he preferred his club; while the attitude of the daughters was perhaps indicated by the statement, in '63, that "modern girls jump at the first offer which presents but a bare living in order to escape from home worry. . . ." but, too often, there was no offer at which to jump. Even in 1860 the probability of a girl's marrying was calculated to be at the age of 21, 1 in 3; at 25, 1 in 6; and at 30, 1 in 16.

With so many competitors and so few prizes a girl must need to jump quick, and the crinoline costume was adapted for a more passive attitude. All through the decade the new phenomenon was discussed on all sides. Thus, in '61, *The Times* expressed the view that the increasing number of unmarried daughters in the professional classes was due to the higher standard of life, and later marriage-age of men. "A man's career is smothered by a happy marriage and a large family."

Everyone had striven so hard to raise the standard of living, and now were unanimous in blaming it; and no one could suggest a cure for this state of well-being. How suggestive is that letter in the Correspondence Column from Lizzie "who is now 25 and has never had an offer; she fears she is getting old; what *is* she to do?" That was, indeed, the question which, at the end of the '60s, a quarter of a million single women between the ages of 20 and 40 were asking; what on earth was a girl to do with her life?

It was a critical moment in the progress of the 19th century woman. Up to this point women had been united in claiming to replace Man's uncertain Favours by established Privileges; but having become the Privileged Sex the invading hosts hesitated—as victorious armies are wont to do. Some were satisfied to hold the conquered territory: others were for pushing on to Man's capital and securing absolute equality with him; while the more timid were alarmed at the success and longed to retreat.

Indecision with furious squabbles between one group and another marked the '60s while Man perceived too late his tactical errors in surrendering education, privilege and freedom to his insatiable foe. But now that the enemies' ranks were divided might it not be possible to form an alliance with the least offensive section and so defeat the schemes of the more aggressive? For

the rest of the century that was to be his
diplomacy. From now on women were divided
into two groups: the Perfect Lady, satisfied with
privileges guaranteed by Man, now her ally; and
the Intellectual Woman, eager for independence
and equality, and waging a persistent war against
the masculine stronghold of political and
economic power. With the former group Man instinctively ranged himself, but not quite wholeheartedly; he found it convenient to play off one
against the other as occasion arose.

The intellectual group was as yet small in
numbers, and its increasing contempt for the
merely fashionable type of woman led it into
strange vagaries which afforded endless opportunities for public ridicule. It is unfortunate that
reforming spirits are so often distasteful people
with queer, unpleasant habits, which the modern
psychologist would explain as signs of sexual disharmony; but in the simple Victorian creed
deviations from the normal were immoral and
the herd fell upon them with tooth and claw.
The way of the reformer is hard, especially if she
be a woman, for she has broken the rule that
females must keep in the herd.

But in the '60s it was the Perfect Lady herself
who was causing so much anxiety; for it seems

that having won her privileged position and emerged into the world, she was uncertain where to turn. Indeed, it was a characteristic of the 19th century woman, admirable as a tactician, to lack strategy. After each victory she hesitated. Always after Cannae her impulse is to turn to Capua.

Extravagance, luxury, and ennui among the "leisured class" was the feature of the '60s, so that a magazine of '67 remarked: "The predominating mood of womanhood to-day is boredom. Has Society in breaking down certain time-honoured restraints which defined social intercourse with salutary strictness over-reached itself? It looks very like it. We live so fast that we have no time for anything. Is it that these great changes are made by a few men who give their labour to the real work of the world, while Society, and in particular women, take no part in it, but merely regard its results with languid curiosity? Society in England boasts of the liberty accorded to young girls. A few years ago it was the fashion to be 'earnest,' an affectation just as everything else is affected. We are drifting without religion or the domestic virtues. Girls have no notion of the seriousness of life and brides have not the faintest intention of fulfilling the sober duties of matronhood. It has become the fashion for reputable Englishwomen to paint their faces and tint their eyelids, to wear false hair and supposititious tournures. Present fashions are hideous, preposterous and injurious to the real attractions of their votaries. Marriage has become unpopular in 'Society,' given up to pleasure seeking, exaggeration and materialism."

In short, the hind let loose was having a high old time.

But what was so specially regrettable was the behaviour of young women of the upper class. These were too young to have experienced the wholesome discipline of the '40s; indeed they looked upon that dreary period of domesticity with that peculiar scorn which the rising generation feels for the day before their own. It is a function of young women periodically to provide their elders with a text for homily and satire; the young lady of the '60s, like other young ladies, was ready to oblige, and she had learnt to use her faculties in a manner that alarmed her elders. Immense efforts were made—as they always are made—to check the innovations of the rising generation; the result was, as always at such times, a vast deal of noise, great self-satisfaction to the critics, and a general sense that the moral tone of the Nation had been thereby saved, while Youth imperturbably and inevitably grew up.

For our purpose it is worth while resuscitating some of the more pungent criticisms directed at those young ladies of the '60s; we see at least what the elders thought they were like. Besides they would form useful models for future occasions, for there was a quality of peculiar acerbity in the journalism of the '60s which is lacking to-day. Whether this was due to a keener sense of style or because the victim was unable to retaliate, it is difficult to say.

It had become the custom to describe the pleasure-seeking young lady as "fast," and fortunately a contemporary magazine supplies us with a precise definition of the term. "In the sense now applied 'Fast' is an Americanism and extremely vulgar, as are all Americanisms. A fast young woman has an inordinate love of gaiety, a bold determined manner, a total absence of respect towards her elders, and sometimes even towards her parents; a flippant style of conversation and a glaring and sometimes immodest dress. She is not in the least sentimental; she does not read Scott or Byron or Moore or even Lord Lytton. In the country she

is a daring rider; in town she plays billiards. Her
conversation is full of slang—so repulsive in a
feminine mouth. We actually know of a young
lady of fifteen who talks about being 'squisshy'
and of a gentleman having 'D.T.s.'" This deplorable habit is ascribed to a pernicious system
of education and improper reading (which are
always the recognised causes of these convulsions
in the young).

But to taste the full richness of Victorian in-
vective against Youth we must turn to the long
series of articles which appeared in the *Saturday
Review* in '67 and '68. They supply an example
of journalistic sadism, in perfect keeping with the
spirit of the day. Their underlying policy (apart
from selling the paper) is obscure, for they abuse
the Husband-Hunter and the Old Maid
impartially; they lash the frivolous and the
earnest and approve of only one sort of woman,
the Hutch Rabbit.

In an article, "Foolish Virgins," the Society
Girl is thus sketched: "After three months of
egregious dissipation the fast sisterhood enter
upon three months of deadly ennui. The pains
and weariness of moral crapulousness arise in
proportion to the passion of debauch. The
shamelessness of apparel, reckless abandonment

of manner, unblushing tolerance of impudent speech characterise the half-dressed Mænads of the Season."

. . . A fine volley of words, gentlemen, well shot off. . . .

The woman of fashion is thus described: "A white or spotted veil is thrown over the visage in order that the adjuncts which belong properly to the theatre may not be immediately detected in the glare of daylight; and thus, with diaphanous tinted face, large painted eyes, and stereotyped smile, the lady goes forth, looking much more as if she had stepped out of the green-room or from a Haymarket saloon, than from an English home. But it is in evening costume that our women have reached the minimum of dress and the maximum of brass. The female bosom is less the subject of a revelation than the feature of an exposition. A costume that has been described as consisting of a smock, a waistband and a frill, seems to exceed the bounds of honest liberality. At the Opera two gentlemen were heard remarking on such a costume. 'Did you ever see such a thing?'—'Not since I was weaned.'"

On the other hand the Intellectual Woman is equally repulsive; "She entrenches herself in the

'ologies; adores Mr. Kingsley because he is
earnest; takes up the grievances of her sex; pro-
nounces old men fogies, and young men intolerable. Her character, like her face is rigid and
osseous; she plunges into science and cuts her
hair short to be in proper trim for Professor
Huxley's lectures."

The same authority points out the cause of
both these dreadful variants from the normal:
"We deny women the direct exercise of their
capabilities and as a result they run to artifice."
As for the remedy, the *Saturday Review* did not
hesitate to enunciate it in one of those concise
sentences which help to solve social problems.
"Man has become a woman-caressing animal; it
is woman's business to charm and attract and to
be kept from anything that may spoil the bloom
of her character and tastes."

The culmination of this series of articles,
which were arousing immense attention both in
this country and in America, was one entitled
"The Girl of the Period." This provoked such
a tempest of fury in the magazines for ladies, and
in newspapers sympathising with the Fair Sex,
such shouts of approval in clubs, such shrieks of
disgust in boudoirs, such articles from Professors
and sermons from Bishops, that the massive

dignity of the Victorian Age seemed to rock and sway; in fact it never wholly recovered its equipoise for it perceived that the Girl of the Period was a portent of a new historical epoch.

It must be confessed that to a modern ear the famous article reads a little tamely; its thunderous indictment is perhaps somewhat in the 'Ercles vein; but we must read it as they did in those decorous days, when the first signs of the Revolt of Woman seemed to recall the horrors of the French Revolution.

"The Girl of the Period is a creature who dyes her hair and paints her face, as the first articles of her personal religion; whose sole idea of life is plenty of fun and luxury; and whose dress is the object of such thought and intellect as she possesses. Her main endeavour in this is to outvie her neighbours in the extravagance of fashion. She has done away with such moral muffishness as consideration for others. Nothing is too extraordinary or exaggerated for her vitiated tastes. With purity of taste she has lost also that far more precious purity and delicacy of perception which means more than appears on the surface. What the demi-monde does in its frantic efforts to excite attention she also does in imitation. If some fashionable dévergondée en evidence is reported to have come out with her dress below her shoulder-blades, and a gold strap for all the sleeve thought necessary, the girl of the period follows suit next day, and then wonders that men sometimes mistake her for her prototype. This imitation of the demi-monde leads to slang, bold talk and fastness; to the love of pleasure and indifference to duty; in a word, to the worse forms of luxury and selfishness.

"The girl of the period envies the queens of the demi-monde far more than she abhors them. No one can say of the modern English girl that she is tender, loving, retiring or domestic. Love, indeed, is the last thing that she thinks of. But she does not marry easily, for men are afraid of her and with reason. . . . It cannot be too plainly told to the modern English girl that the net result of her present manner of life is to assimilate her as nearly as possible to a class of women we must not call by their proper—or improper—name. If we must have only one kind of thing let us have it genuine, and the queens of St. John's Wood in their unblushing honesty, rather than their imitators and make-believes in Bayswater and Belgravia. All men whose opinion is worth having prefer the simple and genuine girl of the past, with her tender little ways and bashful modesties, to this loud and rampant modernisation, with her false red hair and painted skin, talking slang as glibly as a man, and by preference leading the conversation to doubtful subjects. . . . All we can do is to wait patiently until the national madness has passed, and our women have come back to the old English ideal . . ." and so forth for a couple of columns. It would be indelicate to draw attention to its shocking insinuations—made more so by the use of French words. No wonder Victorian matrons gasped and rushed to their dictionaries to discover the exact meaning of the insults.

That this view of the Girl of the Period was not confined to a single journal is indicated by similar diatribes culled from other contemporaries. Thus: "The Girl of the Period is made of Belle metal, three parts brass. Everyone talks of everything nowadays and respect for youth is as much out of date as reverence for age."

"In the new Art of Love the youth of both sexes make advances with about the same impetuosity as an oyster. Is it because our damsels are over-familiar with the swains?"

"Owing to the growing disinclination of men

CROQUET. By W. Thomas. 1865 (?)

to marry, early marriage is not now the natural inheritance of women."

"The world has become so confirmed in its vices, so accustomed to the desecration of passion to a base use, that it cannot see anything in it but vice."

"There is no dignity or real elegance in the short costume and tight jacket now worn by fast young ladies who seem to abjure the sweet dignity of womanhood in a shooting-jacket and a Tyrolese hat."

On the other hand "the matron of to-day quite eclipses the maiden; she flirts more industriously; she waltzes more violently, and she dresses more outrageously."

Phrases like "the disgust and antipathy aroused by women to-day," become hackneyed, combined with alarming accounts of the indelicacy of fashionable costumes. "The low-necked dress and bold look of the wearer are signs of the present fast, frivolous and indecorous age" (1867); and two years later—"they are really wicked, those ball-dresses, wicked for cost and indecent for cut; with only a little gold strap across the shoulders, that look as if a good shake would shake them off altogether."

We seem, in fact, to be reading a contemporary

account of the Decline and Fall of the British Empire by some Victorian Gibbon, until we discover that these hideous practices were mainly confined to that small and not very important section of the community known, in those times, as the "Upper Ten Thousand," which—like an ornamental top-knot—decorated the outside of the thinking part.

But it suggests a revival of Exhibitionism, as a revulsion from that excess of Gothic sentiment which had marked the preceding period. Whether a mere swing of the pendulum or an indication of the unrest in the social fabric which was beginning to be feared by the Leisured Classes, this phase of Exhibitionism was short-lived, and did not extend far down the scale; the upper-middle classes clung to the habitual attitude, and the magazines for the young ladies of that section supply the evidence. It is true, *The English-woman's Domestic Magazine* of 1866 recognised that early marriage in this class was unpopular owing to the cost of living, and commented on the relaxation of social caste which was apparent; while a similar publication stated: "The women of our race are often censured by foreigners for wearing costumes too gaudy and rich—dresses so gorgeous as to attract the eye, so that a truly modest woman would sink into the ground with shame." In 1867 *The Queen* admitted that "the relations between rich and poor are becoming very different from what they were; the working people no longer look up in admiration to those above them in station." But it is in those invaluable mines of self-revelation, the Correspondence Columns of the Ladies' Magazines, that the true voice of the simple English maiden is heard. Its thin sweet pipings reveal the Attitude of Hope —or Hope deferred—the Attitude of Despair, of shy longings and promptings, inspired by the instinct of Sex; sometimes of Instinct withered into strange shapes to which the moderns give ugly names; while those stony-hearted replies, uttered in the voice of Authority, reveal the Attitude demanded by the Herd.

Isabel wishes to know "how she may captivate and enchant the heart of a loving and pious young gentleman"; the oracle answers: "Let her be, herself, loving and pious."

"Wood Violet is anxious to encourage a bashful gentleman to propose," and is advised to welcome him with smiles, invite his opinion as to the books she should read, and adopt the style of dress and colour which he prefers.

Another asks "Do we approve of Confession?

There is a young curate of whom she is dotingly fond, such a clever man, to whom she would like to make her confessions . . . and do we approve of Celibate Clergy?"

Margaret, less spiritually minded, wonders whether "it is right for a gentleman to look wicked"; it appears she is just sixteen.

A more complex problem is presented by one who says: "I am nineteen and am told that a woman should never own she loves a man even if she promises to marry him as it lessens his respect for her. If I receive a proposal and the gentleman asks me if I love him would it be improper to answer 'a little?' My Mother told me of the rule about not 'telling her love,' but my Aunt says it is all rubbish; but *she* ran away with Uncle when she was seventeen so I don't suppose she knows."

A more sprightly Miss who considers "she is very witty" is warned to eschew that dangerous accomplishment for "a man would as soon think of marrying a tigress as a young lady affected with this disease."

"Sweet Briar" is consoled with the news that "some gentlemen are rather nervous about asking Papa, but if they are too nervous to speak they can write, which answers the same purpose."

The Revolting '60s

It appears that Susan is torn with misgivings: "Is it improper for lovers to kiss at parting?" It seems unsatisfying to be told that "a lover's privileges ought to be able to bear a Mother's eye."

If it were not cruel to dissect these palpitating young hearts it would be easy to demonstrate the crude sexual urge hampered by unwholesome restraint until, in many cases, it became converted into definitely pathological forms. Such were displayed in a lengthy correspondence in the columns of *The Englishwoman's Domestic Magazine* for 1868 on the vexed question "Ought we to whip our Daughters?" The volume of letters on this subject became so great that at last the magazine had to publish a special monthly supplement to contain them.

They supply us with evidence of a mass of sadism existing not merely in girls' schools but in the happy English home. Letters from victims as well as from parents and mistresses supply precise details, the number of strokes—twenty to fifty—required "to convert a wicked and stubborn nature into a sweet and loving disposition"; the method—by strap, slipper or birch—(but the birch is preferable "as causing the more exquisite pain"); the tying down or the hanging up (for each has its advocates) of the victim, whose age runs from four to eighteen; the preparation for the ceremony, the stripping and the struggles and the screams; while the executioner (so often a female who has missed the more normal forms of sexual gratification) assures us that she does it "as evidence of the tenderest love." A widower, inconsolable for the loss of his dear wife, explains that "he is now forced to flog his daughters himself, and the elder ones make such difficulties." A lady, boasting of great experience in such matters lays down the dictum: "Unless a Mother uses her authority in this way she loses all hold over her children, and when fear and reverence cease then good-bye to all affection."

When sadists are eager to proclaim their proclivities in public we may assume that the community itself is inclined that way; and whenever sadism is rampant it is certain that obstacles are being opposed to the normal gratification of the sexual instinct. The orgy of sadism in the upper-middle class during the late '60s and '70s tells its own tale.

There is a similar psychological significance in the revival of tight-lacing which started again in the middle of the '60s. A long discussion on its pros and cons appeared in *The Englishwoman's*

Domestic Magazine and elsewhere. We are not concerned with the arguments urged against the practice, mainly hygienic, but rather with the arguments in favour of it. That the practice was widespread is indicated by a letter from a school-girl, in '66, describing her boarding-school as "Whalebone House Establishment," where stays were compulsory and were sealed up by the mistress on Monday morning, to be removed on Saturday for one hour "for the purposes of ablution." It was found possible, by such means, to reduce a waist of 23 inches, at the age of fifteen, to 13 inches, by the age of seventeen. Abundance of "finishing schools" support the practice which ensures a ladylike appearance so necessary in these days; mothers urge the advisability of making daughters sleep in their stays which, we are assured, "carries no hardship beyond an occasional fainting fit." But the psychological significance of this curious custom is betrayed by various ladies who are addicts. One states: "Everyone must admit that a slender waist is a great acquisition; the so-called evils of tight lacing are so much cant. To me the sensation is superb and I am never prouder than when I survey the fascinating undulations that Art affords to Nature"; while others more naïvely inform us that "tight-lacing produces delicious sensations, half pleasure, half pain," and emphasise the peculiar thrill obtained. Against such arguments what availed the warning that "by the practice of tight-lacing the redundant material is pushed up into parts of the frame which become frightfully augmented," or doctors describing post-mortems on its results? The pleasure we delight in physics pain, and distorted instincts assume ugly shapes.

We find at this period that the correct conduct towards the opposite sex overshadows every other branch of ladylike behaviour, for by the '60s they were all young ladies, but some—alas!—were fast young ladies. On the vexed question whether it was quite nice to Waltz, we are told: "The Valse, as it is now called, is an old favourite, but many believe that a lady should never come into near personal contact with any gentleman not a near relative or an actual or probable husband; no dance exercises so great an influence over the senses and doubtless it should be indulged in with caution by all very sensitive organisations." On the other hand "there is no danger in a lady walking by herself in Regent Street, or even in the Parks, *in the day*, if she walks quickly and dresses modestly"; and a correspondent who complains that gentlemen *will* stare at her so, is advised that as there is no law to prevent it, it is better for pretty women to wear thick veils when walking unattended.

Praiseworthy efforts were still being made by Editors (or perhaps Editresses) to check young ladies from indulging in modern practices; one such is curtly informed that "the articles you enquire about *are* manufactured but we decline to state where they are to be bought." "At a recent public assembly every third woman seemed to be painted and eyebrows and eyelashes coloured and false hair worn. If young ladies seek to make themselves attractive to gentlemen by such means they will get no reward." We are told that "the amount of embroidery put upon underclothing nowadays is sinful; a young lady spent a month in hem-stitching and embroidering a garment which it was scarcely possible that any other human being, except her laundress, would ever see"; and that "ladies are making much greater use than formerly of a variety of applications for the heightening of their charms."

We cannot entirely blame the correspondent who complains: "I think you preach a great deal too much about goodness; when it would be far more amusing to hear of some new way of doing the hair. Be good-natured, do, and tell us how to look fascinating, or at least good-looking. P.S. Are chignons likely to get cheaper?"

A milder complaint comes from Mary who "would be so glad to have the magazine give a little news of the fashionable world; she is so fond of the Princess of Wales and the Court, but her Mamma will not allow her to read the papers."

The merely inquisitive young woman is well represented; "Pussy," for example, "adores Tennyson and thinks everything he writes is delightful and is sugar bad for the teeth and what is good for a moulting canary?" While the pure-minded girl informs us "I have never read one of Miss Braddon's novels and hope I never shall; writers of such horrid sensational tales have but little consideration for the nerves of their readers."

For in the '60s Miss Braddon and that horrid Ouida were undermining the morals of the British Empire; provoking a critic to exclaim: "Women novelists choose for their heroes muscular roysterers, profligate guardsmen and dissipated fox-hunters." Young ladies were torn between the attractions of these visionary heroes and the concrete—if slightly pallid—charms of the neigh-

bouring curate. For the pale young curate in the
'60s had an immense following. It was all very
well for sneering folk to speak of "Woman's new
religion, Curate-Worship," but after all, he was a
bird in the hand. As a spinster confesses (in '68)
"The position of a single woman of thirty, in the
middle class, is horrible. Her cares are to be
properly dressed, to drive or walk or pay calls with
Mamma; to work miracles of embroidery . . .
but for what? What we want is something to do,
something to live for. . . ."

Better be a curate's wife; at least there would
be abundance of children.

Signs of dissatisfaction with the social scheme
of things creep into the correspondence columns,
in spite of rigorous censorship. Ellen complains
that she is not permitted to do as she likes and
"Papa's homilies on idleness are a dreadful bore."

For it must be confessed that home life, in the
middle class, *was* a little dull. The house was un-
inspiring. A magazine of the early '60s advises
us how to furnish the drawing-room. "A Brussels
carpet contrasting nicely with the wallpaper
which should be elegantly patterned with flowers;
green curtains draped with white lace; Utrecht
velvet chairs, sofas and Ottoman; tablecloth of
crimson rep with green border on a round centre

table. Ornaments should be plentiful and choice books of travels in an ornamental book-case supply an air of refinement. An oval pier-glass, gilt, with scroll and lattice work; handsome vases of potichomanie on the chiffonier and brackets; and wax flowers in alabaster vases give a lightness to the chimney-piece."

It is a comfort to learn that the cost of all these luxuries need not exceed £40.

The dining-room must strike a more serious note: "two easy and twelve dining-chairs; table, dinner-wagon and sideboard (richly carved); Etruscan water-bottle and glasses on the sideboard; bronze ornaments; marble clock, candelabra and groups of birds in bronze; steel fender and irons; damask curtains, and a rich carpet of a dark hue." In such surroundings one could feed heavily. A man's room, perhaps? . . . And we are advised to forbid the presence of books in bedrooms, especially in the servants', "lest a practice of reading in bed be indulged in; the Bible, however, should be at *every* bedside."

A home obviously conducted on the highest principles, but one which young ladies might find a little lacking in thrills. There were, of course, those agreeable evenings spent in the family circle, when "light or fancy needlework form a suitable recreation for the ladies, varied by an occasional game of chess or backgammon. And nothing is more delightful to the feminine members of a family than for one of the gentlemen to read aloud some good standard work or amusing publication, especially if he is willing to explain the more difficult passages and expatiate on their wisdom and beauty."

Or, with a larger audience, a little music might be indulged in; we seem to catch a faint echo of it in that man's letter of '67: "How any man can be got to stay in some of our drawing-rooms when 'a little music' is going on I cannot imagine. Is it absolutely necessary that so many sisters, cousins and spinsters should display their musical abilities?" It was from homes of this sort that thousands of middle-class young women in the '60s were trying to escape. The governess problem was still unsolved. In 1860 the Home for Unemployed Governesses received 24,000 inmates, in one year.

This craving for an alternative career needed stern reproof. "Young ladies," we are told, "should not be on the look-out for profitable employment but should leave that for their humbler sisters; we have a horror of strong-minded women. Surely there are enough of domestic duties to give women all the scope needed for their abilities." The masculine view was definite enough: "At the present time, 1868, highly educated women will be utterly incapable of domestic management. The proper relation of the sexes will be reversed and Man will be made to feel inferior."

But if in middle-class homes there was a good deal of futile beating of wings against social bars, in the outer world there was an immense stirring. Intellectual culture was spreading among a small but growing group of women who were detaching themselves from the more conventional circles and were studying the political, theological and scientific problems of those restless times. But theirs was, as yet, a world of its own. A more widespread influence was at work, and with it must always be associated the names of Florence Nightingale and John Stuart Mill.

Miss Nightingale, the most remarkable Englishwoman of the century, had not only opened the windows of England; she was teaching women a new principle of living: how to exercise their faculties without emotion, and how to co-operate for an impersonal object. She employed the military qualities of discipline and co-ordination and instilled these novelties into the feminine mind. Unconsciously she was training Woman how to win rights. No wonder that a ladies' magazine remarked that "the tone of her writings shocks our idea of good taste."

In a different capacity Mr. Mill, by his writings and speeches, was demonstrating what those "rights" should be. He indicated the objective; Miss Nightingale drilled the raw troops. Each in their respective way was helping to destroy the conception that Woman was the Privileged Sex. The principle of the Perfect Lady and her proper functions had been exactly implied in a magazine of 1860: "The part women are taking, in the present day, in ameliorating the moral and social condition of the poorer classes, deserves respect. In this work the Bible plays an important part."

It was that sort of attitude which would have provoked the contempt of Miss Nightingale and Mr. Mill. To their mind it was not the Poor that Woman had to improve; it was herself.

She was certainly changing in her appearance. The aloofness of the enormous crinoline was an undemocratic arrangement which could not long withstand the march of events. From about '63 it began to shrink and become flatter in front; in keeping with this, the skirt was gored so that the bulk of it now hung at the back. Woman was, in fact, showing signs of stepping out. The walking dress shortened and revealed not only feet but ankles; and not only ankles but petticoat. A garment thus exposed to masculine eye supplied a sense of delicious embarrassment, and the red flannel petticoat of the period doubtless expressed the feelings of the wearer; it was found that the human monolith positively possessed limbs asking for admiration, and their boldness made the chaperoning petticoat blush scarlet.

In 1867 an observer remarks with complacence: "We never remember seeing so many red flannel petticoats in the streets as this winter."

It seems these short dresses performed immense execution on susceptible males, whose faith in feminine anatomy had for a generation been severely taxed; now at last was the justification of things hoped for, the evidence of things not seen. The new fashion helped to explain the extraordinary popularity of the game of croquet, a paper remarking in '67, "One of the chief reasons of the pleasure men take in the game is the sight of a neatly turned ankle and pretty boots. It is a highly decorous form of flirtation in a pleasant disguise."

It was characteristic of that period that

although young people of both sexes were mingling much more freely together in their social amusements, they never could do so without sex-consciousness; an undertone of flirtation was ever present, for each sex was as yet incapable of regarding the other in any other light.

The design of a woman's costume became progressively more sex-conscious. For example, the bathing-gown had been, till now, a shapeless disguise; but in '67 "the new Zouavemarine Swimming Dress for Ladies secures perfect liberty of action without exposure of the figure," consisting of a short blouse or tunic with waistband and wide trousers fastened at the ankles— made of blue and white flannel and described as "quite coquettish."

For it was so important, in those times of keen competition, that physical charms, though indicated, should not be too recklessly cheapened. But with dowries diminishing and men less prone to marry, the girl without intellectual attractions had nothing to rely on but the allurements of anatomy. Those who dared to steal a march on the rest were very properly censured as "Fast," and those who hesitated, as slow.

The happy mean was adopted and the lady

stepped discreetly forward so that the dress now began to take up a position at the rear; as she walked she seemed to drag her dress behind her, bag and baggage, for the crinoline was no longer a circumvention, but an afterthought, sustaining billowy masses heaped at the rear; as its shape changed into a "crinolette" it carried in addition an enormous Bustle, so that the whole centre of gravity of the dress was shifted backwards. Instead of standing passively surrounded by an impregnable fortification, the Woman had boldly advanced, as it were, to meet the foe.

It was indeed a novel policy from which the more timid shrank. So that many clung to their cages long after the more enterprising had left their crinolines behind them.

It is scarcely necessary to add that the new mode of sex-attraction alarmed the older generation (always so easily alarmed by new variants of the game they used to play). In '68 one complains: "At the seaside most of the young ladies are thinking of the admiration they hope to excite, and reveal it in the mincing airs they assume at the approach of the opposite sex."

The device of the hitched-up skirt to reveal the allurements of the petticoat was so successful that the new revelation became more and more elaborated, both in fabric and colour. It became, in fact, a new kind of skirt over which was then worn a short "over-skirt" or tunic, hanging down in front like an apron below the knees, and cut away at the back. The under-skirt was heavily bordered with quilling, and trailed away behind like the wake of a ship (for the short walking dress was not for matrons whose ankles had lost their charm).

The colour sense displayed during the later '60s was significant. The dress was clearly designed to catch the eye—and the man—by its arresting contrasts of hue. Discordant clashing of colours imply a psychological disharmony; woman was entering a new and difficult phase and was uncertain of her aim. From in front she appeared a veritable woman; from behind she displayed nothing but a dress; she brought her charms forward to meet you, but in retreat was as elusive as ever, for all you saw from behind was a head swollen at the back with a lump of false hair in a net, the Chignon; while below, the Bustle and the Crinolette burlesqued the anatomy of a camel. It was the struggles of an instinct to free itself from a convention; the instinct had burst out in front and the convention trailed behind.

From the middle of the '60s onwards for the rest of the century we can detect in the style of Woman's dress the same contest, the same expression of a want of harmony. It was an epoch in which Curves dominated the essential shape, curves sometimes repressed in one part and swelling out in another, for the curve is a graphic symbol of femininity, and whenever Art has shown a strong inclination to its exaggerated use, it is safe to deduce a sexual impulse denied more normal methods of expression.

The Epoch of Curves in women's dress, occupying the last thirty-five years of the century, indicated an unsatisfied sex-instinct. Formerly the sexes had been, in the main, segregated, and early marriage had supplied a fairly satisfactory solution of the problem which now arose. It would have been extraordinary if an instinct so powerful had not protested against the attempts made to repress it; under those conditions an instinct will find expression in an unconscious burlesque of the forbidden subject, and the dress will display grotesque exaggerations of the normal curves denoting the sex of the wearer. The protest is mutely inscribed in the fashions which characterised the Epoch of Curves.

Chapter VIII

The Ornamental '70s.

DEMOCRACY had now established itself as the system to which, for better or worse, England was wedded. The Reform Act of '67 had shifted the balance of power further down the social scale; while the collapse of the Imperial regime in France and its succession by a Republic was a practical demonstration of democratic progress, the lesson of which had its effect in this country. It seemed necessary, in Mr. Lowe's phrase, "to educate our future masters."

The effect of the National Education Act of 1870 remained to be seen. Would the People be satisfied with knowledge, or would they demand, as its corollary, Power? The Upper and the Upper-middle classes were dimly aware that their supremacy was drawing to its close. Trade began to deteriorate, while the cost of living was steadily increasing. "Meat and coal cost double the price of twenty years ago" (1873). Under the combination of these circumstances it was difficult for the "comfortable classes," especially those on fixed incomes, to retain their former confidence. The stream of legislation emitted by the Liberal Government, from '68 to '74, seemed to disturb the very foundations of Society.

If the decade of the '70s be examined closely it will be seen that the general attitude in the first half differed in many respects from that in the second, for it took some years for the effects of these changes to become established. At first there was, as a writer remarked in 1870, a feeling that "we have thrown off the quiet life and the whole nation is in a ferment;" later a cloud of depression followed.

So far as the higher ranks of the social scale were concerned it will be convenient to consider each half of the decade separately, but the distinction was less evident in the Middle class where change is always slower. But it is the Middle class which now deserves the greater attention because of its power in the State; its political influence still predominated and its moral influence was portentous. The impulse which it had derived from the preceding thirty or forty years had sufficed to establish its lead; and it continued to exercise its power by force of habit. It supplied, more and more, the politicians, the members of the professions, and of the merchant class (as distinct from the tradesman.) It was a class which had prospered at the expense of those above and those below, and it had flourished long enough to have well-established traditions. It was not interested in land (which was unprofitable) or in genealogy (for its family tree was obscure) or in the finer shades of Debrett (except as an imaginative exercise); in these respects lay its distinction from the Aristocracy. But it was profoundly interested in Capital, the slow but steady accumulation of which was the creed of the middle-class male. It was not enough to make both ends meet; it was a moral duty to save and invest. It was this which distinguished the Upper-middle from the Lower-middle class.

The women-folk, too, had their distinctive attitudes towards wealth; the tradesman's wife was perhaps actually helping her husband to make his living; at least she had a keen sense of the cost of making money; but the merchant's wife had slight acquaintance with her husband's business and the wife of the professional man had none; she did not see money being made and her attitude towards it was as something to be spent, prudently or imprudently, for she never saw the savings. The woman of the upper-middle class came, therefore, to regard the actual making of money as slightly vulgar, and a familiarity with that aspect of the subject, as "lower-middle class." It was a sign of the Lady to affect ignorance of the husband's income, or at least to conceal the figure from the world. But she cultivated the art of spending it, and made that the test of good breeding. To be extravagant was vulgar; to be parsimonious was lacking in self-respect. As a Lady she could not afford to look mean, but she might practise sly little economies so long as they were invisible. In truth, the Lady of the Upper-middle class in the '70s was frequently hard put to it to meet the expenses of her position which was poised in a hazardous balance. Unlike the Aristocracy or the Lower Orders, she was liable, through some financial loss, to slip down the scale out of her set; or, if fortune favoured her husband, she might be called on to soar upward into the "leisured class," or a daughter might make a good match—a title perhaps—and she would be in a new world.

Thus she lived in an atmosphere of uncertainty. She was always conscious of her moral tone—that at least was a certainty—and she derived comfort in testing it against those of her set; any wide divergence would imply either she was becoming lax (a dreadful thought) or that those others were "not quite nice" (a more usual but still very unpleasant thought). In a word, her Herd instinct was peculiarly sensitive.

At the same time she was alive to the significance of the outside world: its problems and cultural fashions, which she carefully studied in books and newspapers. Whether her knowledge of humanity was derived from *The Nineteenth Century*, or from Mrs. Henry Wood's novels, it was equally second-hand, for her acquaintances were too similar to herself to supply anything original; nor would it have been welcome, for it was so important to do and think and be precisely the same as they.

Her critical faculty was keen but narrow, and aspects of life were comfortably divided into black and white. Without imagination she lacked sympathy; her standard of conduct was defined; there was but one, her own, for which her feelings served as judge; she *felt* that a thing was nice or nasty, good or bad.

She was quite unaware that in this unreal existence she was but acting a part. Towards her husband, she had a special attitude, no longer servile and no longer one merely of privilege, for by now she had Rights forced upon her. She was his refining influence, sustaining or even raising their joint rank in society, and it was by *her* efforts that their children would (D.V.) rise on the stepping stones of their dead parents to higher things. As the spending partner she had to employ a good deal of ingenuity. An expensive school for the children, or an expensive dress for herself, were equally settled, in the long run, by the exercise of "feminine tact." Of course, it was impracticable to be quite frank towards him, for a man could not be expected to appreciate fully the devious little ways of his better half, nor did he attempt to; while she was perpetually conscious that she was on a slightly higher moral plane with its own moral code. The attitude is indicated in a woman's magazine of 1870: "Some women of refined nature are constantly shocked at being compelled to associate with the coarse-grained animal Man, and their moral sense revolts against the instances of vulgarity found in some gentlemen." It was a feeling shared, to a less degree, perhaps, by every nice-minded married lady, for it seems that most gentlemen were, in some respects, men. It is noticeable that the magazines of this period contain in their correspondence columns a new feature, namely, letters from wives revealing the horrors of married life. Thus in '71, we have an extreme case: "I have borne for twenty-two years with all humility and gentleness of spirit all the insults of a coarse nature. I have been a devoted slave to the man I swore to love and obey: I have borne insults and hard work and words without a murmur, but my blood boils when I see my gentle innocent girls tremble at the sound of their father's voice."

The novelty lies in the fact that such a complaint was written and published. No wonder the Editorial advice was: "As he is the bread-winner you must bear it with a meek and quiet spirit," and other correspondents, perhaps more fortunate, send "a word of remonstrance for such a violent letter against a husband."

There is a good deal of evidence that marriage as an institution was experiencing one of those periodical phases when its failure seems more conspicuous than its success. It was part of that hostile attitude which the sexes had recently assumed towards each other as the result of the campaign in which women had won such signal successes.

The Queen, in '73, comments: "There is a

small amount of friendship existing between men and women; underneath the conventional surface of politeness is a deep undercurrent of enmity. The strange fight that has long been going on between the sexes about the various professions to which the latter has laid claim, testifies to the truth of this. When women cease from being lovers, when they shake off the yoke of submission, and range themselves side by side with men as equals they become at once rivals and enemies. This outbreak of women against men has been both strange and pitiful. One great cause is that women do not care to study men so as to understand them and expect too much personal attention from them. They expect their husbands to tolerate all their habits: their costly and incessant changing of fashion, their powder and cosmetics, their monstrous erections of dyed and false hair, their padded figures, every rounded line made by milliners and none by nature."

Women began to discuss, in the magazines, aspects of married life which hitherto they had reserved for the tea-table. One frankly tells us: "The quiet serious unattractive men are the deep earnest thinkers; such is my experience of twelve years of married life shared by a quiet ugly man,"

—but whether his earnestness or his ugliness was the chief attraction is not stated.

The married woman was developing a life from which her husband was detached. The "five o'clock tea," and the "at home day" were innovations of the '70s, together with, in certain sections, whist parties from 5 p.m. to 7 p.m., in all of which men took little share; and as a result a new feminine attitude developed.

The Times, in '73, declared: "It is a lamentable fact that the gentler sex have a good deal to do with that ruinous extravagance which introduces all the vices and ruins all the virtues; they dress at a rate far beyond their incomes; they are such creatures of rivalry and display that they cannot help feeling a sort of triumph over those who are less fortunate."

In addition, a noticeable feature among married women of this class was the increased consumption of alcohol, the price of which can be gauged from a contemporary statement that "two bottles of sherry, two of champagne, one of port and one of good claret can be obtained for under £2." We are also informed that "many ladies take eight glasses of wine, four of them port, with stout twice a day and brandy and water at night." The point has this significance that women usually take to alcohol mainly because their sexual lives are disharmonious.

The '70s marked the beginning of the decline of those huge families which had been the rule since the Industrial Revolution a generation or so earlier. The economic factor, the wider interests, and the greater luxury were doubtless the chief causes, but we must add another, a frank distaste for monotonous maternity as a career.

In '77 a notorious trial attracted enormous attention. Mrs. Besant and Mr. Bradlaugh were sentenced to six months imprisonment for publishing a medical work on Birth Control, as being "subversive to public morals." The book was condemned by all nice-minded married ladies, but their eyes were opened, and the birthrate in that class showed henceforth a remarkable decline; after all, deeds, not words, are the true test of sympathy. It seems not unreasonable to conclude that the information supplied a long-felt want, for it was being found that the large family had certain disadvantages.

The cost was perhaps the most obvious to a generation experiencing a steady rise in expenses and an increasing difficulty in marrying off daughters.

But there were others only dimly realised. A

paper in '78 discussing the relationship of sisters, remarked: "Family affection was the continuance of the tribal feeling, but now in our own time this value of the family is lost. We do not help each other so much as we divide. Often a set of sisters breaks up into parties; there is jealousy, such as of a younger sister's marriage, or of an elder's privileges." And reference is made to the habit of two sisters forming an unhealthy friendship, "one always in the position of a superior and the other inferior, thereby militating against either's ever marrying." There is, too, a guarded statement in *The English-woman's Domestic Magazine* of '71. "There is not the slightest doubt that England is hastening towards the border which divides the sexes; already persons have over-stepped it and stand alone, hated and despised."

It seems that the huge Victorian family was not seldom a whited sepulchre; it had been a recent innovation; formerly an enormous infantile death-rate had balanced the excessive birth-rate, but with a reduction of the former and none of the latter, the family became of an unwieldy size; tolerable only so long as early marriage of the elder children could be counted on to deplete it.

But the big families of the '40s–'70s period produced a mass of psychological morbidity. In the first place it led to a grandiose conception of "the family" and its ramifications into first and second cousins, with an exclusive family conceit. In the second, there was no privacy for the individual, who was surrounded by family quarrels, jealousies and favouritisms inevitable in such an establishment. Always there was one at least condemned as the inferior, in looks or brains, while the youngest was branded for life. The amount of "inferiority complex" created by these conditions must have been enormous. A further aspect were those unwholesome alliances between brother and favourite sister, with distortion of the normal instincts. Always there was that nameless creature, "Mother's right hand," the unmarriageable daughter, whose fate was to nurse her ageing parents into their tomb, and then retire to Leamington as a decayed gentlewoman. The big family, in fact, was a breeding ground for disharmony, narrowness of outlook and perpetuating family faults, kinks and defects of character, for it encouraged imitative habits and checked originality.

It was one of the factors of that sense of disharmony which was becoming a feature in the '70s.

IN SUNDAY BEST. From an engraving by Edmund Evans

The Ornamental '70s

It is noteworthy that *The Englishwoman's Domestic Magazine,* in '77, has a cautious article on "Have we too many children?" Of course, a negative answer was given which signified less than that the matter was discussed at all in such a respectable family periodical, which incidentally revealed that the maternal death-rate in confinements among the better classes was 1 in 200; so that in order to have ten children, a mother would incur a 5% risk, while 10% of infants died in the first year.

It was all very well for the charms of maternity to be preached to a woman by non-combatants such as the *Saturday Review,* whose article, in the '70s, on "Womanliness" informs her that "she knows that part of her natural mission is to please and be charming; she knows she was designed by God and by Nature to be a mother, sent into the world mainly for that purpose, and has no new-fangled notion about the 'animal' character of motherhood."

It came, by a happy coincidence, at the very moment when Bismarck was also proving that the male was designed by God and by Nature to be cannon-fodder.

It was the custom to shield a girl from any knowledge of the physical aspects of marriage; as a fashionable physician of the day so neatly put it to the mother of an engaged daughter: "Tell her nothing, my dear madam, for if they knew they would not marry."

But the Divorce Act had led to a revaluation of marriage, and women were becoming more critical of masculine conduct. They inevitably came to despise the masculine demands which were to be tolerated only as a duty, and hence arose the feminine notion that all physical functions were derogatory to a refined mind, and that the Perfect Lady should be as ignorant as possible about them. A girl who ventured to ask her mother the meaning of the word "abdomen" was told that it was quite unnecessary for a lady to know, as it was something only found in the "Lower Orders." And *The Queen* (1870) remarks: "So long as women think it improper to have any knowledge of the structure of their own bodies, so long will they be incapable of understanding the evils of tight-lacing."

If the correspondence columns of the magazines for ladies are examined, we find that the replies to medical questions reveal a singular fact: that in the '70s the well-bred lady never suffered from any disorder between the diaphragm and the knee, except "the liver," which seemed to occupy the entire space between those limits, and was regarded, for some reason, as a perfectly ladylike organ. If there *were* other structures within the Victorian lady, they were nameless. See, for instance, the reply to Louisa: "To your first question, if you have a good home do not leave it merely for excitement; to your second, try charcoal biscuits." From which it appears that all was not well with Louisa, but what? Some deep depression in the domestic circle?

Articles on Health for Young Ladies were received by readers with distaste. Indeed, Emily complains that they "make it very awkward to leave the magazine about in case my brothers should see it." But occasionally some persistent questioner receives a blow below the belt; Dolly, who keeps asking: "What is the probable cause of my always having flushed cheeks?" is finally silenced by: "A disordered stomach"—but such ungentlemanly rejoinders on the part of the Editor are fortunately rare. That they had, in those days, some sort of anatomy, is, however, revealed by the illustrations, which were beginning to appear, of articles of underclothing. But these, when bifurcated, are pictured only in a folded-up state (evidently symbolic of the mental attitude of the wearer). The very garment itself acquired a sinister reputation, for it betrayed the nature of Woman's understanding; no wonder a "Rector's wife" writes an indignant letter to deny that either she or her sisters have ever worn such things.

It was the feature of the '70s to conceal facts, or at least to disguise them by ornament until they were unrecognisable, so deeply planted was the Gothic principle; it was the fashion, in refined households, for common objects to be ornamented into strange forms; the dinner bell must be draped like a statuette; the match-box should look like a castle; the waste-paper-basket is hung with frills, and the thermometer encased in scroll-work; a gentleman's braces are enriched with floral patterns in Berlin wool; we are offered illustrations of "an embroidered spittoon," and an "ornamental stand for tooth-picks." Your toilet set would resemble a flower-garden, and some, in a spirit of loyalty, would ornament the interior of the humblest utensil with a portrait of Her Majesty.

From top to bottom the house was ornamented. The dining-room, for instance, "should have a crimson wallpaper with a dado three or four feet from the ground, in the form of a narrow shelf holding small china ornaments and odds-and-ends which will take off the stiffness; family portraits in oil on the walls, a black sheep-skin rug and a Turkish or Brussels carpet with the floor border stained brown. And too much furniture is a mistake. A table, two deep arm-chairs, and a dozen ordinary covered in leather, a sofa, sideboard, dinner-wagon, occasional table, writing-table, a bookcase or two and a screen are quite as much as are necessary." Here one partook of ornamental sustenance; a lady describes a little luncheon for eight as comprising "Lamb cutlets and peas, quails, cold lamb and beef, chickens, ham and tongue, veal pies, jellies, iced pudding and apricot pastry and other light articles of that description, with strawberries and cream. It was *perfect,* especially the sherry, of which I partook of I don't know how many glasses."

This spirit of ornamentation found equal expression in the costume. During the first half of the decade Fashions borrowed their ideas from the age of Louis XV, and Propriety, garbed à la Pompadour, concealed the body and betrayed the mind, for the craving to attract was surging beneath that ornate surface.

The Chignons, "those wonderful structures of frisettes and hair, either growing or borrowed, which women are now in the habit of rearing on their heads"—at the cost of 30s. to 60s. each—were said "to impose such a weight on the heads of these martyrs that they deserve pity rather than reproof."

The frisette, or substructure, had an extensive sale; in 1870 a single firm was turning out two tons of them a week.

Nor did the face escape ornament: "No one who goes much into Society can fail to notice how common the use of paints, powders, and cosmetics has become of late years" (1871).

As for the dress, "Toilettes imitate the Louis XV style, with looped-up skirts, aprons and tunics draped with large bows. The tournure, of white horse-hair, arranged in a number of puffs, is worn over a scanty jupon which has only a few steel circles round the bottom; two skirts, one plain, the other flounced, are worn over it. Flounces by themselves are not sufficient trimming and must be completed by fluted headings; never were trimmings more elaborate than now." The tunic was now open in front and hung down behind; the Pagoda sleeve returned to fashion for small hands were in great demand. The foot, too, was a feature of sex-attraction. The high heel produced a peculiar tilting forward of the body which fashion described as "the Grecian bend." The purpose of the high heel is revealed in the comment (1870): "It causes the muscles of the calf to be in a state of permanent contraction and the result is—no calves." (And thin ankles.) These allurements are graphically described in '73: "Of late years fashions have greatly improved in elegance and taste. The tight-fitting jacket shows the dainty little waist; the looped-up skirt displays the feet in pretty high-heeled boots; and a fullness in the skirt behind and at the hips gives grace to the figure and makes the waist look smaller, and is a development of that contour which is universally considered a great beauty in the female form." The corset, besides its effect on male susceptibility, was found to have a moral function. "It is an ever-present monitor indirectly bidding its wearer to exercise self-restraint; it is evidence of a well-disciplined mind and well-regulated feelings"—a happy contrivance, therefore, to inflame the passions of one sex while restraining those of the other. A similar motive seemed to underlie the use of some of those more intimate secrets of the toilet. "Patent elevators for the figure" (as advertised) had their functions, as may be gathered from an answer to an enquiry: "If Annie understood how much embonpoint is admired she would not desire to get thin." For the gentlemen delighted in seeing "Beaucoup du monde dans le balcon."

The purpose of it all was plain enough. "If daughters were only usefully employed after leaving school we should not see so many listless young ladies about, whose only amusement is to powder their faces, dress in a conspicuous style, and fancy every young man is overpowered by their fascinations; upper-middle class girls show an absolute ignorance of house-work and dislike it. Unless they are fortunately interested in district visiting, the greater part of their time is spent in altering their costume to suit the ever-changing fashions, and the perusal of cheap fiction. Their walks extend no farther than to some shop or congenial friend. With a capricious appetite their digestion weakens. An enforced return to less artificial needs may do much to check vulgar display and revive that domestic life which is one of the greatest safeguards of English honour."

Those who were strangely insusceptible to such ornamental charms rebuked the woman of the day as "frivolous, discontented and irrational," while an article in '75, entitled "Fashions Run Mad" is very severe: "Dressmakers load their

work with ugly and senseless frills which do not
end anything, with bows which do not tie anything, and with buttons which are of no use, and
are incapable of understanding the grace of simplicity. A dress is considered a perfect fit when
a lady can neither raise her arms or use her legs;
the fashions of the last six or seven years are certainly more picturesque than those of the crinoline days. From the way in which the female
form is made up, from the false hair streaming
over the shoulder, to the toes pinched in high-
heeled boots, throwing the weight of the body with
its enormous humps and hoops on to the toes, the
seeming giantess must surely prove a terrible
dwarf to her husband when divested of her
garnishing."

Evidently a bachelor's letter, for he overlooks
the Etiquette of the Dressing-room, to which the
husband was banished as soon as his spouse
began to disrobe; while in households lacking
the married man's "funk-hole" (into which he
escaped at the psychological moment) it was the
rule for the wife to retire half an hour beforehand
while he waited until a discreet knock on the floor
gave him the "all clear."

There is, unfortunately, a lack of evidence on
the psychological aspects of this delicate subject,

except by inference. Thus in '71, a blushing bride is advised how to furnish the bedroom: "You will need a double wash-stand, a large winged wardrobe, a handsome chest of drawers, good chairs and a pillar toilet table with a mirror. This, with the dressing-room adjoining, will cost £120"—but observe the modest hiatus; there is no bed.

Owing to the disappearance of the crinoline it was remarked, in '70, how ladies and gentlemen were now able to walk arm in arm again, and the novel proximity stirred the man's emotions so that one exclaimed: "It is certainly very gratifying to have a pretty girl on your arm." We can, perhaps, visualise the effect of a close-up from the statement, in '73, "A well-developed bust, a tapering waist, and large hips are the combination of points recognised as 'a good figure.'" Undulating effects were obtained by the Polonaise, and the Dolly Varden costume (of chintz pattern over a cambric skirt) and its hat with those provocative curves, were new and deadly weapons appearing in '72.

It must be admitted there were moments when the charmers might have been caught—or at least observed through a glass—off their guard; for seaside bathing in '72 afforded a poignant spectacle. "Garbed in the hideous blue serge sack called a bathing gown, with hair tightly screwed to their heads or hanging in helpless tails on their necks, they scream, splash, gasp and jump in an insane way at the wavelets and then return shivering to their bathing boxes. About 1 in 50 can really swim; as to costume we are wonderfully behind the world. " But this is a jaundiced—or possibly shortsighted—view of costumes which elsewhere are described as very smart objects "composed of seven yards of twilled flannel, with high neck and long sleeves: some even with body and trousers in one." And in any case they were not meant to be attractive, for the wearers were not, at the moment, thinking of the other sex; they were trying to avoid getting wet. But if they did not always think of the absorbing topic, they sometimes dreamt of it in "a very pretty night-dress, open in front for three inches; trimmed with richly embroidered insertions, and the sleeves demi-ouvert, and very graceful."

But the pure-minded English girl, with her wholesome dread of the foreigner and his wickedness, preserved her charms for home consumption. "Why do English lady tourists take such pains to make themselves frights?" Obviously it was a protective device. For the same reason "young ladies when travelling alone must wait in the waiting-room until the train arrives, and they must not enter the refreshment room, which is not a suitable place for them." Equally necessary was the caution: "A young lady cannot go with her fiancé alone to a party, although a widow may do so."

Owing to the more frequent mingling of the sexes it was becoming more than ever necessary for a nice young lady to be always on her guard. One writes to ask "the meaning of the word 'metaphysics' as she heard it used the other evening and people looked so shocked." In fact, to be shocked was becoming a thrill in an otherwise uneventful existence. The question whether at a dance it was or was not shocking to sit out on the stairs with one's partner was much discussed. In the opinion of one young lady "surely to do so would be excessively fast, in fact, it is one of the fastest innovations of this fast age." She adds: "Where can I get the song, "I would I were a Violet'?"

Theodosia is informed that "to give a pair of slippers to a gentleman to whom she is not engaged would be the height of impropriety; giving her photograph would be most dangerous as no young man can be trusted not to make improper use of it; it might even lead to her being talked

about." Poor fatherless Beatrice, who has been
receiving attentions for two years from a gentleman without his coming to the point, asks:
"Ought Mamma to ask him his intentions—and
is there a cure for blushing?" The answer to the
first question is "No"; to the second, "only by
growing old."

It was fast to attend a skating rink without the
protection of a male relative; it was fast to cross
the road to speak to a gentleman—"unless he is
very old"—it was fast to invite a brother's school-
fellow to tea; it was fast to wear a hat instead
of a bonnet to church; and it was exceedingly fast
"for young ladies to sing comic songs; a lively
ballad, with a sly dash of innocent humour is,
however, permissible." Those drawing-room
ballads have, for us, a profound psychological interest. "Oh! How I wish Mamma was here!" is
recommended by a magazine as being full of feeling and sweet simplicity; on the other hand, "Be
quiet, do! I'll call my Mother!" is said to be
wholly inadmissible, as containing regrettable
features. But ballads breathing a lofty moral
purpose were always appropriate, such as "Lips
that touch Liquor shall never touch Mine."

And yet, in the "Exchange Column" there is
a suspicious tendency to offer bundles of these

compositions for "something useful." Here is Marie, who would gladly take a pair of ear-rings for "Pilgrim of Love" and "Take back the Heart"; while another offers "Thou are so near and yet so far" and "What does little Birdie say?" in exchange "she does not mind what for."

Of their indoor amusements novel-reading was perhaps the chief. In '73 *The Queen* remarks, "For one man who reads a novel there are ten women who make this their sole employment. One constantly meets young ladies whose minds are so saturated with fiction that they talk like heroines; highly wrought descriptions of love scenes are not desirable reading; they suggest feelings which it is undesirable to stimulate." And certainly few could be unmoved by the description of "My Hero," in a novel of that name: "The great dark blue eyes, shaded by black lashes, the straight nose, the curved lips and the pearly teeth, only half-hidden by the golden-brown beard and hair of darkest brown curling gracefully round the Classic Greek head —Ah! that is the man, tall, lithe, strong and beautiful altogether."

The principle is clear which underlies the advice given to a youthful reader: "We do not consider Ouida's novels fit for any unmarried woman." It was the duty of a young lady to get married as soon as possible, but she must on no account experience any passionate inclination towards that state. It was the best way of ensuring a maximum of early unhappy marriages.

Such was the mental attitude of a vast number of young women of the conventional upper-middle class, to whom the pranks of the "Modern Girl" were abhorrent; and we must recollect that the "Modern Girl" has, in all epochs, formed but a small—if noisy—minority; for the great Middle Class has always been the Backbone of the Nation, or at least the part that is always behind.

But there was an increasing proportion of this class who were now being educated and finding careers, in spite of the reiterated warning: "advanced education diminishes a girl's chances of marriage." Or should we say, the *danger* of getting married? There was an immense amount of stubborn opposition. It was still possible for a magazine, in '72, to admit: "the hopeless inadequacy of most of the ladies' schools where only accomplishments to increase a girl's attractions before marriage are taught; at present it is almost a misfortune for women to have aspira-

tions and culture higher than the ordinary level; most women have not yet arrived at the point of realising their ignorance and subserviency, and many are merely gilt drawing-room ornaments."
. . . For it was an ornamental age. But a new milestone had been planted, needing no description beyond the single word engraved on it, "Girton." Its effect can be gauged by the complaint, in '79, of a dining-out gentleman, who writes bitterly of "The Coming Woman"; he had chanced to sit next to one at a dinner. "She was so amazingly scientific and profoundly intellectual that I was appalled. Repelling my ordinary remarks with a freezing stare she started volubly on Comtism, Darwinism and Bathybism"—entirely beyond his powers of digestion.

Likewise the girl of the leisured class was progressing along the accustomed lines, provoking the comment, in '71, "the increasing masculine tastes of the ladies, such as slang and cigarettes," until in '78, "everywhere we see this total change of habits and manners, but in nothing more than the tone of familiarity between the young of both sexes in certain societies. Girls are 'awfully jolly' and young men are 'dear boys' (and parents 'too awfully dreadful'). In the modernised zeal to make themselves so much the companions of men are not women running the risk of losing their distinctive charm?"

It was about now that young women were "slowly awakening to the fact that physical exercise is good for them; they play croquet; they are no longer afraid of long walks and archery delights many; with more freedom of action they have acquired a healthy development and a certain go-ahead spirit which is the sign of the times." (That is to say, of the '70s.) Moreover, we have a description, in '79, of walking tours, for which a young lady is advised to take "two cotton dresses, one cashmere dress, one ulster, one alpaca dust-cloak, one parasol, one umbrella, one walking-stick, one pair of shoes, one pair of button boots, six pairs of stockings, two straw hats, one green veil, and a small flask of brandy in case of faintness."

Bolder spirits were to be seen on tricycles, and there were even projects for starting women's Clubs.

Whatever her station in life, the young woman of the '70s was trammelled with unnecessary impedimenta; whether it was accomplishments or prattle about protoplasm, or alpaca dust-cloaks; they were each representative ornaments. For the same reason the Dolman and the Mantle

229

dripped jet, and plain surfaces were relieved by passmenterie trimming and fluttering ribbons. They were not essentials to life, perhaps, but they ornamented it; to us they betray a fussy, nervous disposition, as of one who is not in harmony with her environment.

A remarkable phase, affecting mainly the more fashionable section, began to show itself about the middle of the decade. Those rococo curves and undulations vanished, and a minor revival of the Vertical Epoch developed. In '74, the back of the skirt was tied by interior tapes so that the main portion became close-fitting to the body, while the caudal appendage trailed behind like a fox's brush.

With these "tie-back" dresses were worn long-waisted "cuirasse-bodices," lacing behind and suggesting corsets put on over the dress; with them stays were unnecessary. The effect was to emphasise the vertical line in front. The tunic was now closely swathed round the limbs so that the wearer was effectively hobbled. The chignon had vanished from the head in '73, and now the hair hung down on the neck in large plaits, resembling a lobster's tail. In '77, we read, "Toilettes have not been for years so elegant and becoming as they are now, the very types of

beauty, gracefulness and style, the Princesse robe
and the robe-habit with the skirt trained at the
back and moulded in front." In the Princesse
shape, which everyone affected, the result was
that of a graceful statue—swathed in wrappings
ready for removal. Odd scraps from the fashions
of the beginning of the century were revived; a
"Directoire habit," an "Empire" bonnet, and the
like, but although the dress was as tight as a
dressmaker could make it, the approach to the
true Vertical principles was but half-hearted.
They could never quite overcome the Gothic dislike for Exhibitionism, and the human frame
never emerged from obscurity.

Nevertheless the innovation was a remarkable
one; it called for a tremendous scrapping of
underclothing to meet the requirements of the
sheath-like costume; necessity is the mother of
invention, and the sheath fashion gave birth to
"combinations," and by the next year "combinations are universally worn." The proud
possessors of that "svelt" form which was now so
desired, resorted to "chamois leather combinations, high in the neck with long sleeves," worn
with a tight chemise and a gored flannel petticoat. . . . .

"A combination and a form, indeed,
  Where every God did seem to set his seal,
  To give the world assurance . . ."

For evening dress further reduction was necessary, and the cuirasse bodice was worn next the skin.

We are not surprised to be told: "The modern gown shows the figure in a way, perhaps suitable for young and slender people but it is certainly most unsuitable for the ordinary British matron," who may have had good reasons for disliking Exhibitionist fashions.

This miniature Vertical Epoch, which occupied the later '70s, was popularly known as the "Aesthetic Period." Already in '75, the Louis XV style of furniture was being replaced by Louis XVI, with its vertical rectitude of form. "Stiff-backed chairs, plain square tables, and baronial bedsteads have become the fashion"; dress was, in fact, simply following the prevailing taste in other arts, as it always does.

By '78, the homes of the "cultured" required complete refurnishing. We are advised to make our drawing-room "with an all-over pattern of paper, or better—in fresco or sgraffito—and it should present one dominant tint in the room

232

to which all others introduced are subordinate.
A black and white Persian rug; Queen Anne
sage-green draperies for the windows; a dado of
Japanese tapestry and a Japanese sunshade in
the grate; 'china shelves' and a blue and white
jar over the door, which has a portière; pottery
on brackets and an eruption of blue plates on the
walls; a high folding screen painted with Oriental
birds; tall palms in painted terra-cotta pots, ferns
in hanging baskets, and a window conservatory
in the Queen Anne style; low chairs of odd
shapes painted black and gold, and artistic furniture, that is to say, either Queen Anne or
Jacobean, if you can afford it." (In those
aesthetic days Queen Anne was a nebulous compound of "Chippendale" and "Empire.")

Unquestionably it was all extremely ornamental
and vertical and intellectual. And in keeping
with it the man of culture aspired to be lank and
dank and limp and obscure; while the aesthetic
female, as seen at a party, is described by a guest:
"A wan, superb-browed woman, with a throat
like Juno, was dressed in a loose yellow garment
and in her hands she carried tiger lilies; gold
Egyptian ornaments clasped her neck and arms;
there was a concentration and stillness in her
movements, and under her wild hair her eyes

seemed to be questioning everything." However, the companion, a young man evidently enraptured, exclaims: "Her dress is the ideal of what a dress should be; its colour, the fall of its folds, are soundless words set to music by herself. She has mastered the art of dress and knows the value of that wild hair which is in harmony with that grand massive chin." A more prosaic description is supplied by a magazine of '79. "It now seems the ambition of the fair sex to confine their locks to the smallest possible dimensions, and the present mode of skirts is supposed to be 'after the Greeks.'"

For the apostles of the new cult were Greek in their looks, Pagan in their emotions, Cinque-Cento in intellect, Queen Anne in their curtains and Japanese in their pots . . . in effect, Super-Ornamental.

The Aesthetic Movement, in reality, was a superficial thing, affecting a small section of the community; psychologically it was a mixture of Exhibitionism and Fantasy, an attempt to escape from depressing realities. Its adherents claimed to be protesting against the blatant ugliness of an unsympathetic world, always the plea of the fearful neurotic. And as Fear is destructive to that Gothic attitude of mind which normally marks the race, so its victims are prone to turn to vertical forms of art for moral support, and derive a pseudo-courage from Exhibitionism. It explains that itch to "shock" the Herd and that craving for notoriety which affects some victims of an "inferiority complex," who, to prove to themselves that they are not the cowards they feel, will strip themselves of conventions and air their naked notions in public. The Aesthetes betrayed their psychology in their taste in colours; a preference for those faint-hearted tints which Nature exhibits in moribund vegetable matter.

Far more interesting was the colour sense of the first half of the decade, when the employment of two tones and two textures in a dress was introduced; it expressed that underlying disharmony which they tried to disguise by over-ornamentation. For Ornament did not mean high spirits but a mask to conceal a feeling of discord.

Woman was dissatisfied with her mental and physical environment; she was perceiving the essential difficulty, how to obtain adequate satisfaction for Instinct and Intellect.

Some were engaged in developing one at the expense of the other, but the problem, for which she could see no solution, was how to develop both.

Chapter IX

The Symbolic '80s.

"AT no time in history have the human nerves suffered as they do now from the wild speed at which life travels, and the pressure of occupations and amusements. Leisure seems to be a thing of the past. It is the age of hobbies and activity; everybody is doing something. It is the fashion to have artistic tastes. . . . How intrepid our ladies are! They visit hitherto unexplored regions, they skim the seas, they ride through the desert; they ascend the highest mountains, and come home and write sparkling accounts of their travels. Not only is it travelling, literature, charity and art that occupy highborn ladies but they plead and advocate causes before the public. The cynical recorder of our age, probing the leading motive that actuated its energies, may declare it to be a craving for notoriety. The more philosophic speculator may perhaps see in the prevailing restlessness that of a generation who having drifted away from the

236

traditions of its forefathers has not yet formulated the code that is to rule its future."

Such was the sagacious speculation of one writing at the beginning of the '80s. It exactly expresses the problem which the Woman of that period had to face, a problem inherited from the preceding decade, and one which she, in her turn, was destined to pass on, unsolved, to her successors.

That a solution of it had not been immediately arrived at was, after all, very natural, seeing that the vast majority, at least, were incapable—and are still incapable—of perceiving the precise nature of their difficulty; they were dimly aware of its existence, but they could not diagnose the disorder with scientific precision.

As indicated at the close of the preceding chapter, Women had begun to recognise the profound difficulty of adapting the normal instincts of sex to the highly artificial restraints of an intellectual environment, and they had followed the most obvious course in dealing with it. They had assumed that sexual instinct (except its purely maternal aspects) was a regrettable inheritance from a savage past, and therefore it seemed clear that its subjection was necessary if civilisation

237

was to progress. But the crude method, at first adopted, of passive silence on the subject (in modern parlance "Repression") was now in the '80s replaced by more promising lines of treatment (in modern parlance "Sublimation") : one being an intensive cultivation of the Intellect, and the other intensive physical training. They were methods which had been introduced, half a century back, by Arnold for schoolboys; they were now thought to be equally suitable for adult young women; we find each being advocated with immense enthusiasm, in the '80s, but without much conscious realisation of their primary object. It was recognised that a vast number of young women were doomed to suffer sexual starvation and it was resolutely instilled into them that this was "the higher life."

As the result of the different courses of training, widely diverging types of young women began to evolve. Thus a writer in '83 remarks: "The life of a young English lady to-day, both in the country and town, is essentially one of exercise; certainly the ladies of to-day can indulge in far more physical exercise than their mothers or grandmothers had before them; the demand for muscular education and amusement has increased rapidly of late." Meanwhile

238

the intellectual young woman, as a result of increasing facilities for education, was rapidly winning successes in various professions, and cultivating proficiency in the Arts and Sciences.

For a time all this seemed to be admirable and sufficing. "Young girls are beginning to realise (1883) that marriage is not the aim and end of their existence. They are no longer content to idle away the best part of their lives in waiting for a future which may never arrive." At the same time, among the daughters of the "leisured classes," a third type becomes prominent. "During the last few years (1885) there has been a decided improvement among girls of the well-to-do class in the direction of sport; two out of three play tennis all the summer; there are no bread-and-butter Misses now; there are no Girls; they are all Young Women. Far from them is all idea of schoolroom ignorance and innocence, farther still all notion of submitting to parental authority. Their Mother is a person whom it is their first duty to get rid of as soon as possible. The Young Woman nowadays marries herself not to the man she likes but to the man she can manage. She knows everything; she reads everything from French novels to the evening papers. For a wager she will dive head-first off a boat or run you a race round Belgrave Square in the middle of the night."

And lagging in the rear of these three sorts of Modern Young Woman there was, as always, the old-fashioned Home-Bird, who clung to the domestic nest with its now slightly fusty surroundings.

An American visitor to these shores in '83 supplies a description which is evidently applicable only to this type: "The English girls are dull, diffident and monotonous; with their pale eyes, pale hair and sealskin jackets one might gather a thousand of them all alike. The English girl utters her little harmless platitudes in a soft low monotone of broken sentences in a limp and watery way; always shy and diffident the conventional attitude never changes; she never stares, never asks questions; she is trained to seem to be a negation, a dormant soul without volition." . . . A perfect picture of virginal repression. And if perchance any attempt were made to rouse her watery passions, her reaction to such an appeal was characteristic; as in a magazine story of '81: "He stooped and kissed her soft lips. The next instant she had snatched away her hands to cover her face whose paleness was succeeded by vivid crimson, while he stood overwhelmed with shame and penitence for his audacity. 'Can you ever forgive me? I know you cannot. My conduct is inexcusable and ungentlemanly; I have only one excuse to offer: it is, that I love you.' "

If only love could be purged of its grosser aspects, how welcome would it be! How to attract in a nice way is explained to an enquirer who calls herself "Kitten." "To be attractive a girl should be healthy, intelligent, industrious, amiable, cheerful and ready to be pleased with small pleasures; this brings an expression which cannot fail to attract in the face of even a plain girl.". . . What more should man want?

With four such distinct types, each with her characteristic attitude of mind, it is not surprising that contemporary accounts of the '80s differ widely. Superficially they seem to be creatures of different civilisations, but beneath the surface they have a quality in common; each is unconsciously seeking to evade the rational claims of the sex-instinct. It is something of which she is afraid.

If she were asked (but, of course, she never was asked), each would have supposed it to be a mysterious impediment derived from our baser natures, tending to drag us down; admittedly marriage might have compensations which made it, on the whole, a desirable state, but the instinct itself had horrid aspects about which a nice girl did not care to think. As a young lady of the period expressed it: "It would be terrible to be married and have to be seen—by a husband—in one's petticoats."

Psychologically, she was suffering from a suppressed Fear, which explains the phenomenon observed by a writer in '87, "the hysteria and neuroses which are the curse of to-day."

The '80s, mistaking a healthy instinct for disease, tried to cure it by treatment which would, no doubt, have been very effectual if the diagnosis had been correct; as it was, it merely created a fresh form of fear, Prudery, which devastated the next decade.

However, for the first six or seven years of the '80s the principles employed seemed to be answering very well; a cold restraint pervaded the Woman of the day; from apeing what she supposed to be the artistic ideals of the classical age she found herself petrifying into the most solid disguise that woman has ever assumed. In the Bustle era, from '83 to '87, her upper half, with close fitting bodice over long tight stays, presented an unbroken surface of concrete which seemed to emerge from a skirt of dense drapery, solidly supported by a metal frame. Was it to indicate her victory over Nature that Woman converted herself into a War Memorial?

Yet, in spite of that air of chilly virtue in her daily life, in the surroundings of her home there was an atmosphere of fidget and fuss; a perpetual rearrangement and finicky adjustments which implied a latent dissatisfaction. Presently, towards the end of the decade, the instinct held in restraint broke out into a riot of sentimental ornament and prettiness.

To the proper understanding of the '80s it is important to realise that in spite of all sorts of wholesome expansion in women's lives, there was something unreal and therefore unwholesome about her essential Attitude. She was afraid of her instincts and was seeking to circumvent them.

And, of course, the man of her day was unconsciously helping in the process, for his position was equally at stake. Together they were trying to build up a new world on a foundation never intelligently explored. Their Art, on that account, is very instructive in a psychological sense, for, as we should expect, it is very symbolic of a restless dissatisfaction.

The "Aesthetic Period" which still affected the

first two years of the decade was beginning to
fail; an escape into fancy dress will not cure a
neurosis. We find, in 1880, the comment: "If the
gaudy red and gold monstrosities of twenty years
ago (a vulgarised Louis XV style) may be
likened to the obstreperous loud laugh, some of
the Aesthetic modern rooms may be likened to
the sour stare; grim and acidulated in colouring, cold and formal in aspect, dotted with heavy
high 'Chippendale' chairs, rickety little tables
and sofas glazed and spotty with inlay—why
are these things called 'Queen Anne?' The
upholsterer attaches the term 'Early English' to
all periods from Queen Anne to Napoleon; to
modern oak settles carved by machinery, everything that looks ecclesiastical, and to all ugly
colours. There are drawing-rooms where the
Aesthetic craze is rampant, where women wear
all kinds of furniture materials for dresses, and
dress their furniture in silks, velvets and
brocades; where women cut their hair short all
over their heads and thoroughly well touzled;
where a blue plate is called 'divine': a Queen
Anne chimney-piece 'adorable,' and a broken tea-
pot 'utterly perfect.' "

But even the enthusiasm of its apostles could
not persuade the British Nation to become whole-

GIRTON GIRLS. Drawing by A. Sandys in the *Lady's World*, 1887

heartedly aesthetic, although it claimed to have produced "that revival of the taste for the artistic adornment of residences which is one of the signs of the times."

And certainly there was an immense desire, on the part of cultured women, to render their homes perfect pictures; but they were not to be realistic pictures; realism must be disguised. Thus, your drawing-room fireplace, when not in actual use, must be hidden, and in the '80s a wide choice of suitable objects are offered for this purpose: "Rustic trellises, baskets, ferneries, grottoes, curtains, fans, Japanese umbrellas, imitation spiders' webs, birds' nests in moss, emblematic shields (either with your crest or some more spiritual insignia), sprays of peacock feathers, stuffed birds and animals, artificial ice blocks, or curios—all are used with more or less success."

But mere disguise was not enough; that had been practised in the '70s; it was now being reinforced by positive concealment; hence arose the passion for draping objects. It was unconscious symbolism; in the attempt to cloak an instinct it was not sufficient to drape her body; a woman felt impelled to drape everything about her.

We are told, in '87, that "draperies give an air

of refinement to a home; on the mantelpiece should be placed an oblong small mirror, bordered with red and gold brocade, supported by a large fan of artistic pale green, and a tall red jar holding pampas grass. Draped material surrounds them, with a couple of pearly Japanese fans above; the mantelboard is covered with green velveteen with a festoon or 'drop' in the centre; short side curtains of the same hang in front of the fireplace jambs, which are to be covered with a rich crimson paper. The wallpaper should be sage-green, and the piano-back, which stands out, may be draped with moss-green plush; on it should stand an Eastern brass pot containing a palm, with a few plush framed photographs, and a china ornament or two, while on the ground is a milking-stool draped with a couple of terra-cotta handkerchiefs, and on it a bowl of pink poppies."

You will then have satisfied the requirement that "a room should be treated with a colour of a pitch sufficient to give some pleasurable excitement."

And you will also have done your best to smother up facts.

Presently, however, "there is an inclination to change the fashion of drawing-rooms to a lighter style; tall screens are discarded for short ones, with delicate looking furniture, elegant tables and beautiful brocades draped over chairs and sofas."

It is the woman's and not the man's rooms which, we find, are being subjected to nervous readjustments. She seems to have been pre-occupied with the subject. "The predilection for artistic furniture may be considered as having taken its place among the necessaries of refined life," remarks a Woman's paper in '82.

How widespread was that interest may be judged by the enormous number of enquiries addressed to Women's papers, asking for advice on this important matter. Indeed, their eagerness for draping their homes seems to have been carried almost too far, and one earnest enthusiast receives the chilly reproof: "No, we do not advise you to drape your ceilings." However, doors, windows, fireplaces, sofas, chairs, and especially bare walls, seemed to invite drapery. For this purpose Oriental fabrics were abundantly supplied by Manchester, or even from the East itself, while Art serge, Art silks, Art velvets and Art cretonnes rivalled the ubiquitous plush. With the best will in the world there were some domestic articles, however, it was impossible to

drape; these could be painted or—better—
enamelled.

"The mania for painting everything, fans,
blotters, wooden barrels, glass jars, mirror frames,
milking stools, beer-jars, three-legged cauldrons,
drain-pipes, etc., does not seem to diminish"
(1883). Drain-pipes, decently disguised by
painted designs, did duty as umbrella-stands,
while milking-stools, enamelled a hedge-sparrow
blue, and tambourines prettily decorated, would
grace the drawing-room. No wonder a lady exclaimed with ardour, "Without my pot of enamel,
life would be a desert blank!"

It is characteristic of symbolic acts that they
never satisfy, and are therefore repeated indefinitely, and it seemed almost impossible to
supply enough novelties to keep pace with the
demand. In '84 we are offered: "A stuffed kitten,
with coloured ribbons round its neck, in a gilded
basket, lamp-shades hung round with stuffed
birds quivering on wires, an imitation coal-
scuttle, gilt and tied with coloured ribbons, to
stand by the fire as an ornament, a real scuttle
of coal being kept out of sight; photograph-frames
with little curtains to draw across, and varnished
bulrushes to stand in draped drain-pipes"—all
very suitable as Xmas gifts for a lady.

The Symbolic '80s

It is true that this artistic fashion met with its detractors—as what Art movement does not?—and someone, in '86, utters a sneer at "the trivial fashion of filling a room to overflowing with trashy articles that can be bought for a few pence; clusters of fans round the overmantel, cheap china and brass-ware; toads, mice and lizards have the run of the bedroom, and boars and cocks and hens in the boudoir. Feathery enormities swing by chains from the ceiling; our ornaments are valueless and ugly, our dress flashy, and our houses flimsy."

Obviously a critic who failed to perceive the subconscious motive of the fashion; those things were but symbols, inspired by an instinct denied a more normal form of expression; the passion for disguising objects, and still more for covering them up, is always a sexual impulse striving to find a conscious outlet.

Another characteristic example of symbolism, especially noticeable in the '80s was the passion for using portions or replicas of dead animals as ornaments, both for the person and the house. A few contemporary comments will serve to illustrate the intensity of the fashion. Thus in '84: "We do not require to go to the Zoological Gardens to see strange animals; we see them on our hats, our muffs, our buttons, our jewellery, and even our dresses. Ask yourself if cats, dogs, mice and monkeys are suitable dress trimmings? What shall we say of a dress trimmed with cats' heads, ditto her bonnet, and muff? The newest thing for the shoulder of a ball-dress is velvet loops with a few white mice seemingly playing about them." And we are given a design for "red silk stockings covered with black swallows."

By the next year the craving for dead birds had become irresistible. "The useless slaughter of hundreds of thousands of beautiful birds for ornamenting women's dresses has recently attracted attention. Modern fashion dictates the most reckless disregard of prudence and humanity; foreign and native birds are slaughtered wholesale and the extinction of many species is imminent. Thirty thousand humming-birds are sometimes sold, at the wholesale auctions, in an afternoon." And in '88 we read, "The senseless slaughter of birds to form ornaments for hats still goes on."

In spite of numerous articles exposing the barbarities inherent in this trade, the fashion persisted; indeed its cruelty merely stimulated the sadistic craving, for it seemed to take the place of those flagellations and funeral-orgies of the past.

When the following decade comes to be considered, it will be seen how the lust for dead animals gradually faded into an innocuous craving for imitation flowers with which to decorate the female form, but the symbolism remains.

It may be of interest, to lovers of sport, to have a record of such game as could be secured, in the '80s, from the person of a fine lady; it would have been possible to gather from her head excellent specimens of dead parrots, owls, humming-birds, pigeons, hawks, larks, thrushes, finches, sea-gulls, as well as birds' nests with eggs complete, beetles, cockchafers, and imitation centipedes, lizards and scorpions, while other parts of her dress would supply dead foxes, squirrels, rats, mice, snakes, and replicas of spiders and flies, together with fragments of bears, wolves, and other beasts of prey . . . which one must give her the credit of assuming had no other attraction but a symbolic.

An orgy of Sadism? Or perhaps to indicate Circe-like powers of turning her admirers into animal forms? Or a starved maternal instinct trying to represent the longed-for offspring by animal forms? They suggest, in that case, a queer taste in children.

A contemporary paper merely states that "quaintness is one of the charms at which we aim."

It would be tactless to look for symbolism in the dog-collar which she loved to wear round her neck, and when she suspended a pair of railway engines from the lobes of her ears, the significance of such ear-rings is still more obscure. Did she, in her subconscious mind, yearn to be just a little —fast?

A more remarkable symbolic feature appeared in the costume of this period, namely, the Bustle, which began to return in 1881, and became universal in the following year. Although we speak of its "return," the new shape was radically different from that used in the '70s. Then it had formed, as it were, an integral curve in the opulent undulations of the dress, and expressed an exaggeration of the sexual features of the wearer. It was therefore a part of the armour of sex-attraction. But the Bustle of the '80s projected, not in an alluring curve, but as a bold promontory, jutting out at right angles from the trunk. As an observer remarked: "Look at the modern camel's hump, whereon a good-sized tea-tray might be carried, or at church your prayer-book." The fashion, lasting in its extreme form till '88, coincided with a style of dress aggressively hostile to the male, at a period when Woman was priding herself that she had discovered careers in which she could dispense with physical allurements.

But yet she must needs drag that clumsy mass behind her! Why? A woman, writing towards the decline of the Bustle period, was so struck by the persistence of that ungainly and purposeless fashion, that she remarked: "There is a curious and deep-seated affection in the female mind for something which drags behind her," and she instances the small girl's liking for dragging an old shawl across the nursery floor, and her mother's pleasure in a trained skirt; but this observer, ignorant of modern psychology, fails to draw the inference: the maternal joy in being able to lead her child by the hand.

The Bustle of the '80s was essentially an unconscious expression of a maternal craving, and the fashion was accompanied by a significant arrangement of the front of the skirt, which was draped as though a further addition to the family might presently be anticipated. Thus will a primitive instinct insist on expressing itself by

253

symbols whenever humanity claims to have "risen above it."

So that the Bustle of the '70s was inspired by the "mating instinct," while that of the '80s was inspired by the "maternal"; and as the old century passes onwards towards the new, this differentiation of Woman's sexual instinct into its two component parts becomes more and more marked. She was beginning, at least, subconsciously, to distinguish between them, and to search for means of satisfying, often only by sublimation, their respective needs.

With this in mind we can distinguish between the symbolism expressing an unsatisfied mating instinct (e.g., the sadistic forms; the desire to cover up by drapery or paint; and the wearing of ornaments having a definite male significance, such as: "a bracelet from which are suspended small images of camel, fox, bear, lion, horse, dog, elephant and rhinoceros") ; and the symbols expressing the maternal instinct (e.g., the Bustle; the ornamental small animal; the "kitten in a basket" type of decoration, the use of which was, significantly, confined to the feminine rooms of the house).

Such, then, was the psychological background of this decade, concealed by the diversity of the foreground; it is hardly necessary to add that the various types of women of that period were supremely conscious of the latter, and wholly unconscious of the former.

Each adopted Attitudes which seemed to them self-explanatory. The Cultured, the Athletic, the "Society," and the "Home-Bird," each type developed her own mode of life, without troubling to wonder why. In tracing their progress through the decade it will be convenient to consider each separately, borrowing as far as possible the comments of contemporaries, whose observations of facts is always so much more reliable than the inferences they sometimes attempt to draw from them. In conclusion we must glance at those habits of mind and body which inspired the fashions common to all.

For one large section of the community it was an age of intensive Culture. Education, for girls of the upper and middle classes, had become general and "at the present time may well be a subject of congratulation" (1883). Apparently for that reason we begin in the early '80s to be deprived of that invaluable source of information, the Magazines for Ladies. As soon as young women began to be properly educated, they declined, apparently, to favour those bland soporifics whose number henceforth diminished with distressing rapidity. The survivors undergo a notable change of policy, being forced to cater for readers of a lower social class. One detects a subtle change in the attitude of such magazines towards the lower orders, who are no longer referred to with the old air of disdain, but are positively flattered. Thus, a correspondent in '80, is given the reply: "We think uncommonly well of you although you call yourself 'but a servant of the lower orders.' We are glad to hear from you. Can you not try to improve your handwriting? Do you pray enough?"

One perceives the hand held out. . . .

While in '84 a kindly disposed lady offers a positive olive branch: "In London servants are generally satisfied with a few hours' outing on Sundays. My own cook is far too respectable to wish to go out in the evenings, but it seems hard that they should not have a little fresh air and exercise in the week as well; when a servant is sent out on an errand she is apt to remain longer than is necessary; there is no excuse for this and she should be severely reprimanded, but it is only reasonable to allow an outing on Bank Holidays, when it is a good thing to encourage her to go to such beneficial places as the British Museum.

No mistress will regret a little indulgence of this kind, for we must remember that servants, like ourselves, have minds and bodies which need occasional rest and recreation."

As a proof of this admirable spirit servants are henceforth to be called "domestics."

In place of the old-fashioned Magazines for Ladies, there was a remarkable increase in those for both sexes, and the weekly papers supply a new feature specially to please their women readers: a bright chatty account of the daily doings (real or imaginary), and the personal appearance (real or otherwise) of the Best People. But it appears that (in 1885) "Good Society in London is now wholly composed of second-rate people, nine-tenths of whom are pushing vulgarians. The restraints of good manners are cast off and they have adopted the gospel of Free and Easy."

As for the remaining tenth, composing the Very Best People, they were suffering from a wasting disease which had become chronic, a Deep Depression in Agriculture and Lowered Rents; and they began to fade away into the background as nebulous phantoms, unless rescued at death's door by blood transfusion from America.

With increasing education young women began to read in all directions, such as to cause the greatest alarm to their mothers, one of whom, in '85, utters the piteous wail: "I can't tell what is coming to the girls nowadays. I was never allowed to read such books; I never talked of such things; why, my mother would have fainted if I had even heard of such gossip as the girls discuss nowadays. . . ." (And it is those bold young things, who, fifty years later, are aghast at their granddaughters.)

It was in vain that papers proclaimed: "There are some novels with which no pure-minded woman ought to soil her fingers; under pretence of fidelity to life, scenes and people are described whose acquaintance few people can make without being a little the worse for it. Our magazines deal unblushingly with subjects that, a short time ago, would have caused them to be banned. Thoughtful girls ponder over questions that would otherwise never have occurred to them, and careless ones revel in sensational stories. This early acquaintance with evil lowers their standard or at least destroys their optimism."

A more liberal view is indicated by a paragraph in '87: "Mothers used to object to their daughters reading *Adam Bede* because it deals with what we should prefer not to discuss. Happily this prejudice has to a great extent died out."

But the craving for draping over unpleasant truths was intense, and when Ibsen's *Doll's House* appeared in an English translation a lady's paper expressed the essential psychology of the period in a single sentence: "Ibsen discusses evils which we know to exist but which it can serve no useful purpose to drag into the light of day."

But they had got so far that they knew the evils existed.

We are assured, in '83, that "the upper middle class Englishwomen are well informed and are companions and friends to the men of the household. From this arises a more sober tone in mixed society and the discussion of graver topics in the course of daily life."

And in '88 cultured young women read *Robert Elsmere* right through.

The Attitude of this type is depicted (in '86) in a lady's paper: "She is highly educated, attends lectures and concerts. She reads Morris and Rossetti and Walter Pater; in lighter moments, she reads Ouida and Miss Braddon, for Dickens is out of date. She learns carving and fretwork and paints on china. She is devoted to her brothers and is an admirable tennis-player. They escort her to places of amusement where she does not attempt to attract undesirable attention. The Modern Girl is dutiful though she is apt to give her parents counsel and reproof; sometimes she has views on politics. . . . She knows quite well what she is about and is absolutely sincere in her likes and dislikes which she is apt to express with considerable candour."

One seems to see a calm, clear-eyed Pallas Athene, terribly chaste. . . .

Her more athletic sister was busy cultivating physical fitness; the mild charms of croquet and curates no longer appealed. Tennis, archery, cricket, and, at the close of the decade, golf, were vigorously practised. We must picture the enthusiastic tennis-player of 1880 in a costume "of pale blue flannel with deep kilted skirt and long basque bodice (over stiff stays); an embroidered apron with pocket to hold the balls, and a long overcoat which is intended to be removed for playing." An arrangement which perhaps explains the comment: "The present healthy custom of indulging in active outdoor amusements is sadly interfered with by the ordinary costume." For even when playing in vigorous games the draping impulse could not be wholly resisted.

In '85 *The Field* informs us that "Lawn Tennis has taught women how much they are capable of doing, and it is a sign of the times that various games and sports which would have been tabooed a few years ago as 'unladylike' are now actually encouraged at various girls' schools. In like manner ladies have taken kindly to certain of our sports and pastimes (shooting, hunting, fishing, yachting, rowing)."

And they were indulging a taste for Walking Holidays; on such occasions "a companion is highly desirable, not so much as a defence against that bugbear to most women, 'a man,' but in case of mishap. For clothing, 'flannel next the skin' should be the rule; beneath a dust-coloured woollen dress the woollen undergarment must come up to the neck and down to the middle of the thighs, with long sleeves to the wrists; this, with flannel drawers and a light-coloured petticoat is all that is needed for underclothing."

But this draped Pedestrianism seems to have been, in the opinion of the more cautious, a perilous adventure; a magazine of '82 utters the warning: "It is not merely a breach of etiquette for a girl to take a country walk alone, it is absolutely unseemly and dangerous. There is always a chance of meeting tramps or drunken men." Yet, in spite of such risks, two ladies, in '84, write proudly to say they have just walked 220 miles in eleven days, carrying only 4 lbs. of luggage, at a total cost of £7.5.0.

In "Society" athleticism was equally fashionable. "Nowadays (1887) there are few girls who cannot ride over a fence in good style, or play tennis, cricket and even shoot, and who can tramp over moors and turnip fields." Already, in '85, it was being said, in reference to this class: "This is an age of independence and we do not fear what will be thought of us if we drive alone in a hansom cab. The *very* modern girl is somewhat gawky; she has brushed back her fringe; she refuses to dance, and her dress is a failure, and she uses no perfume. It is difficult to please her; it is more difficult to shock her, and it is impossible to surprise her. 'She is very difficult,' says her mother; 'you see, she knows so much more than I do. She hates music and does not quite know what she wants.' "

In addition, she was developing a shocking taste for slang. "Ghastly," "Awful," "Beastly," were commonplace terms in '84; more recondite expressions such as "quite the cheese," and "gone a howler" provoked the remark: "The use of such terms is vulgar and foolish, and girls using them should be sternly rebuked. Worse still, they call men 'fellows' and even speak of their Father as 'the Governor.' It is sad to see that good manners are dying out."

But happily this mannish phase began to disappear towards the end of the decade when the Gothic principles and Attitude of mind once more asserted their supremacy. We have seen how, in the earlier years of this period, the various types of young women although pursuing widely different paths had this feature in common; they displayed a noticeable indifference to the arts of sex-attraction. It is significant that cosmetics were scarcely advertised; it was as though the women were too busy developing their lives physically and intellectually to trouble much about being "charming." Yet the instinct was there latent, as it were, for it could be detected even in the most unpromising material. "The modern girl who speaks in a loud and strident voice; sticks her arms akimbo: is rich in slang and goes in for Women's Rights: yet has a waist of eighteen inches and wears a hat that would make up into two, with a small barrow-load of flowers piled up on it in front."

The feature, then, of the first half of the decade, was an apparent indifference to sex-attraction.

If we now turn to the end of the decade we get, in '89, a totally different picture: "What a charming majority of English girls we have! Sweet girls, so full of life and hope, so full of the lovely follies of their age! How like the living flowers they are! What a sense of sunshine and purity they bring with them! Suppose that a broad anecdote has been circulating—once the girls come into the room the whole thing vanishes like smoke; not the coarsest man would repeat that anecdote before the girls. . . ." And we are offered portraits of three typical sisters: "Yetta is tall, graceful, shy, quiet, with music as her prime accomplishment, and love of home and home life as her personal quality. She conquers her inborn timidity so far as to make herself useful handing cups of tea, till her fair cheeks deepen into the colour of a monthly rose and her big blue eyes become yet darker and more humid under the flush. The curly-headed Fenella is a B.A., a dainty little soul with her sensitive temperament and active intellect, but her health and nerves have suffered by the enormous strain of her studies. Was it worth it? . . . Beatrice is now the young matron without ceasing to be the pure and gentle creature of her earliest youth; still those glorious eyes like soft brown moths which shine with unabated affection." A striking change, surely, from the beginning of the decade, and one which has a curious resemblance to that which took place in the '20s, when the Classical Attitude of the Vertical Epoch was transformed into the Romantic Attitude of the Gothic.

And if we turn to the costume of the '80s we find precisely the same change, for the "Aesthetic Period" was, fundamentally, Classical in spirit, with a vertical emphasis in Dress and Art; indeed, a magazine of '80 claims that "we are returning to the fashions of 1811."

It is perhaps necessary to add that, in the '80s, they were extraordinarily distorted from the original models so that only certain features can be detected; the preference for long vertical lines is there, but the corseted low waist produces a queer burlesque of the Classical style. And instead of an air of confidence, there is a fussy nervousness. The hobbled skirt, with rows of narrow flouncings and flat pleatings, is a sort of caricature of the skirt of '18–'20. The "Mother Hubbard" mantle is a weak imitation of the cloak of '20–'21. The vertical spirit seemed half-hearted and a change towards a more Gothic style can be detected as early as '82. The front of the dress, in spite of its vertical drapery, revealed a liking for long sharp angles and ponderous curves. There was, indeed, some alarm lest the swing of fashion should bring back the wide skirts of the Crinoline Period, and, in fact, such a movement started to appear, with one or two steel hoops round the bottom of the skirt; but the democratic spirit of the times would never countenance the huge pretentiousness of a full crinoline and the movement got no further.

For a few years, from '83 to '86, Fashion was frozen into immobility, and the Gothic impulse held in check produced one of the queerest shaped dresses of the century. "No one can maintain that the steels now inserted into the backbreadths of the skirts can in any way improve the set of them; they wobble from side to side with the most ludicrous effect," heightened, doubtless, by the excrescence of the Bustle, and three large poufs at the back of the dress. "From four to six pounds is not an unusual weight for a dress."

There is, perhaps, always something a little comic in humanity's affecting to ignore its instincts.

The Symbolic '80s

We have an American's comment, in '83, on the general effect: "Englishwomen are the worst dressed, except perhaps the Germans. Good taste is conspicuous by its absence; in form the English dress is dowdy, and in colour frightful."

The explanation is indicated in the comment of another observer: "When Women recognise that dress is not the great object of life they will have done much towards assuring the alteration of their social position which is the aim of so many to-day."

In fact, they had already recognised it; hence their dress. Sex-attraction was for the moment suspended; they were otherwise engaged.

"All dresses are made in a simple—even severe —style; perfect fit being relied on to produce the 'mannish' style which is, unhappily, the prevailing taste" (1883). Perfect concealment was enhanced by the Tunic which "now hangs down in front below the knees and is draped at the sides; or a polonaise draped at the sides and reaching nearly to the ankles" (1884).

The uncompromising appearance was emphasised by the fashion for tailor-made costumes, and by a singular high-crowned hat, popularly known as "three storeys and a basement." It was futile for a paper, in '85, to protest that "the spring bonnets are hideous! But which are the most hideous, the bonnets or the hats, is an unanswerable question."

But how unjust a criticism! Women's fashions can never be hideous; at their worst they are merely appropriate to the feminine Attitude of the day.

And the fashions of the early '80s were peculiarly appropriate; they suggested a bevy of celibate Police-women.

About '87 the insidious Gothic spirit could no longer be held in check. Just as the mind was becoming unmistakably sentimental and romantic once more, so too the style of Dress. The Bustle shrank into a mere pad; the rigid surface of the bodice was covered with lace trimmings and fichus; ribbons decorated the costume, attached to shoulder, bodice and skirt, while a coy bow encircled the neck. The severe tight sleeve expanded into puffing and epaulette; the drapery was modified by a host of "pretty-pretties" in the way of trimmings, and trailings, and the hat took on a romantic breadth, faintly recalling the joyful haloes of 1827–28.

The colours were now borrowed from the garden and imparted an irresistible air of sweet girlishness.

If, too, we venture to explore beneath the surface, we find evidence of sex-attraction stirring;
mysterious allusions—"false hips and false busts
are now being worn; the Padded Patent
Regulators impart any desirable fullness of surpassing beauty" . . . one supposes, some thrilling device for the undoing of Men.

They were accompanied by a yet more
startling innovation: Romantic Underclothing.

Thus, in '89, for evening wear, "a thin, silk
petticoat, a fine embroidered chemise or silk combinations; a fine silk vest worn next the skin;
under the corset a long and short petticoat; the
prettiest of underclothing is a feature of present
fashions, with the revival of embroidery." And
in '88, elaborate petticoats with "baby ribbons"
run in and out of the flounces afforded a mute
appeal. The effort to be "attractive" did not stop
there; indeed, the more elderly were alarmed at
"the excessive nakedness of modern full dress,
which is a pain and often an embarrassment to
those who observe it." (Depending, possibly, on
the sex of the observer.)

"The lowness of the bodice and the absence of
sleeves leave an impression of nakedness which
makes more than the prude and the old fogey
uncomfortable. But we have improved beyond

269

all measure in our colours and harmonies; half-tones of delicate shadings make a party of ladies now like a flower-bed of loveliest colouring; what a pity we cannot have dress for age! But so long as stays are to be had with sufficiently strong laces, who will not try to appear like sweet Anne Pages instead of being female Falstaffs of formidable dimensions."

Well might a critic in '88 remark: "Never was the art of Women's dress so thoroughly studied or so brilliantly carried out as in the present day."

In a word, it was once more becoming sex-attractive.

At the end of the decade, just when a sentimental Attitude was reappearing, the dress-designers thought fit to revive the "Empire" style. It was, of course, anything but the psychological moment for such a style, and it is interesting to note how it was only accepted after it had been deprived of its essential features; that is to say, the vertical effects were gracefully obliterated or softened by pretty little Gothic touches. Thus one saw: "A toilette of white gauze, ornamented round the skirt with rows of satin ribbons, a gathered skirt and draped bodice, white satin bow and streamers round the waist, and puckered elbow sleeves"—the whole mélange labelled "modified Empire."

But do what they would the dress-designers could not make the sentimental Englishwoman accept the high waist; and so she compromised with a broad sash swathed round the figure to conceal its un-Empire level; an excellent instance of Instinct's vanquishing the dress designer. Whereas vertical lines had been acceptable at the beginning of the decade they were rejected at the end, for the mental Attitude had changed. Instincts which had been, as it were, imprisoned, now emerged as the new decade approached, and demanded attention. The '90s seemed to offer a prospect of sentiment and spring-time after the long winter of the '80s.

The world of the '80s was not happily arranged for romance; amongst other factors the persistent economic depression made it, at least for the majority, one of the gloomiest phases of the century. That this by itself was not sufficient to explain the dreariness of Women's fashions is shown by comparing them with the fashions of the '40s when economic conditions were equally severe but fashions were cheerful because the average woman was then in harmony with her environment.

One hears, all through the '80s, the monotonous cry of "lowered rents and depression in trade and agriculture." It is significant that in '85 the birth-rate sank to 23 per thousand, a lower figure than had been seen for thirty years; while in '88, the marriage rate was the lowest on record, and the marriage-age steadily rising. It is worth noting, too, that the number of divorces had risen from 200 in '68 to 400 in '78 and 450 in '87.

It was found, as always, difficult to reduce the accustomed scale of living and representative figures reveal some extravagant items; thus, on an income of £1000 per annum, a married couple with two servants were spending on dress £122, rent, rates and taxes, £160; and on wine and cigars, £68.

Another couple, on £400 per annum, gave the figures, "rent, rates and taxes £70, dress for both, £60, wines and spirits £22."

Intemperance was rife in all classes, the death-rate from that cause having doubled from 1860 to 1880. We are told, in 1887, that "intemperance exists to a frightful extent among educated women; one of the causes is the grocers' licence" (introduced in '61). It would be more correct to ascribe it chiefly to the psychological disharmony

resulting from the long drawn out battle of the
'70s, by which Woman had won her "alternative
career," and was now tasting some, at least, of
the fruits of freedom; she was fundamentally
dissatisfied, for instinct whispered that she had
lost as much in one direction as she had gained
in another. She viewed the "Shrieking Sisterhood" and their demands for more Rights with
some distrust; were they, perhaps, leading her
sex astray?

The problem is approached by a writer in '88:
"The desire of the young woman to appear
slim and anti-matronal has something of the
irresistible force of an instinct. A retrospect of
fashions is a saddening study; in its ever present
absurdity where is the place of reason, where the
hope of improvement? Where the evidence that
women are not a race of fools, bound hand and
foot by invisible forces? Look where you will,
there will you find daughters longing to make
their way in the world, feeling the want of
definite occupation and the intellectual power
which they have no scope for using"—and at that
point the psychology of the '80s stopped. The
conventional Attitude towards the sexual instinct was the barrier. The firm belief that in
Women at least a normal instinct is a vice was

deeply planted in their minds. Their modern world had put early marriage out of reach; it was disquieting to be told, as in a magazine of '80 that "at thirty a woman is not exactly venerable though her girlhood is past and gone," and with it all chances of utilising her chief gift; it became but a buried talent. For the married woman it was equally something not to be recognised as such. When, in '83, a campaign was in progress for repealing the Contagious Diseases Act (dealing with prostitution) it could only be described in a lady's paper as: "The C.D. Act dealing with a subject of which all respectable and decent women must of necessity be totally ignorant"; for on all matters sexual their minds were swathed in drapery.

They had, in fact, adopted a draped Attitude which showed itself in their clothes, their thoughts and their homes. But somewhere buried out of sight was a restless instinct that was not wholly reconciled to the new world.

Chapter X

The Prude's Progress in the '90s

PRUDERY is an exaggerated Fear of the sexual instinct.

The Prude is necessarily highly sex-conscious, so that the dreaded subject is detected in a thousand innuendoes, in inanimate as well as animate forms, for a multitude of objects become, to the Prude, symbols of it.

But the Prude differs from the Ascetic, who has trained his mind away from the subject; whereas the Prude is continually training his (or hers) towards it. He does not admit, of course, that the subject fascinates him, but in fact he derives a peculiar satisfaction in detecting those symptoms in others which he professes to condemn. And unlike the Hypocrite, who only professes, the Prude does genuinely shudder at sex; the explanation being that subconsciously he longs to indulge but fears to do so.

Prudery, therefore, is an Attitude of mind in which excessive sexuality and fear are essential

275

ingredients, and it was the Attitude which dominated the '90s.

We have seen how, towards the end of the '80s, the normal sentimentality of the nation began to show itself, together with a revival of the normal instincts. There was a resemblance, at first, to that similar revival which had occurred in the '20s, but now conditions were very different. The "early marriage" solution was no longer available, and Woman was taught to repress or deflect the feelings which were trying to assert themselves. A minority, by way of protest, tended towards Exhibitionism, while an intermediate group were endeavouring with more or less success to sublimate their unsatisfied instincts by physical or intellectual careers. It will be observed that none of these three types were in a state of psychological health.

The Prudes formed the largest, or at least, the most important group; owing to the growing economic rivalry between the sexes there was a sense of hositility; the average woman was facing a new kind of competition; not merely that of her own sex, but that of the other as well, for Man was no longer a creature to be won by the exercise of her sex-charm, but an unscrupulous rival in business with a host of unfair advantages. It was

A PICNIC. By Ernest Prater, in the *Lady's Realm,* 1897

inevitable that she should regard him with increasing Fear.

And yet she was aware that a mysterious quality in her make-up might at any moment paralyse her fighting powers and cause her to surrender to the dreaded call of sex. It would have been strange if, under these circumstances, she did not approach the great unknown with a sense of ill-suppressed nervousness; and yet it held out immeasurable fascinations. Rich with Gothic sentiments, she longed for some purpose to which they might be put, but she shrank from adventure. To be Romantic, as in the '30s, needed a degree of courage which she lacked, so she drifted helplessly into an Attitude of sentimental Prudery, torn by distant Hope and present Fear. Some clung to the shelter of home, but an increasing number found themselves thrust by hard economic facts into an unsympathetic world charged with danger.

Prudery is an Attitude of mind which betrays itself in speech, appearance and conduct. In the less sophisticated and simple-minded, Prudery will show itself in all three ways for they are too naïve to wish to conceal it; so in the '90s the lower-middle class displayed the feature in every possible way. Indeed Prudery became synonymous with Respectability. The more educated women, however, were forced by circumstances to mix with men in a business world under conditions in which the usual sex-attitude was apparently suspended; they found themselves jostled by men rivals, criticised by men as masters, measured one against the other by tests which were no longer based on a capacity to attract; in brief, they were called on to employ their minor gifts and not their major. It was not easy to lay down weapons which had served them so well in the past.

They were trained on the supposition that the majority would never experience a fully satisfied sex-life and that therefore it was something on which their minds had better not dwell; it was wiser, indeed, to regard it as a peril to be avoided, and that "Purity" is the happy panacea. But a powerful instinct is not to be fobbed off with platitudes, and with an enormous number Purity was no more than Prudery. The '90s displayed a peculiar appetite for Purity, and hungry zealots haunted the streets and music-halls, longing to discover vice; there was, indeed, a reverend gentleman who charged a young woman with the crime of 'accosting" because she had addressed him with the shocking words: "Hullo, Bertie!

Why d'you look so sad?" The magistrate's comment that it seemed to have been a very suitable remark, gave the campaign a serious rebuff.

For it seems to be a feature of the Prude never to look quite happy, as indeed hungry people never do.

It was natural that a certain minority in the '90s were conscious that this Attitude was morbid, and as a protest against it, they swung violently over to the opposite extreme and practised various forms of Exhibitionism.

Thus the '90s provided these principal attitudes: among the less educated a conscious Prudery; among the more educated, either an unconscious Prudery or Exhibitionism. All are forms derived from an interference with the normal development of the sex-instinct.

These various Attitudes characterised the greater part of the decade, but a noticeable change began to show itself in the last couple of years, reaching maturity in the "Edwardian" days of the present century: a swing-back in the direction of more obvious and normal forms of sex-attraction. It was as though the instinct refused to be held in check any longer.

Of the above-mentioned groups, the first was mainly supplied by the Lower-middle Class and was, of course, numerically the largest. The Lower-middle Class Mind, such as it is, is mainly composed of traditional feelings. It is isolated from the ranks above by a lack of imagination, but in the '90s it was no longer isolated by ignorance. Popular education had supplied it with one supreme blessing; it could read the newspapers and ascertain exactly what Their Betters were like; what they were doing in the fashionable world, and what they were saying; it was impossible for the Aristocracy to get a smut on its nose or on its character without a paragraph recording it. An enormous appetite was encouraged and fed by this means, so that readers came to learn that "Society" was a very shocking institution, and that it was much better to be out of it. They learnt, too, the evils of wealth, and that the sex-instinct, unless carefully controlled, inevitably led to the Divorce Court.

"Sex stories" have always a wide appeal, and readers of the Press derived a great satisfaction from peeping, as it were, through the keyholes of other people's bedroom doors. From the rather limited view thus obtained the Lower-middle class mind (which, of course, is confined to no particular section of the community) came to regard the sex-instinct as something **very** depraved but at the same time the peeping Attitude supplied satisfaction by proxy. The Prude could also obtain a thrill from the mere association of ideas; thus, a correspondent who had had what might have been a real adventure is consoled by the reply: "Your having slept in a hotel alone, by accident, brings no disgrace on you, for you seem to have acted discreetly in remaining in your room." Clearly she had been trained to believe that there is ever a Lion in the path, and she had actually been all night in the jungle. . . . A similar spirit is shown in the answer: "A servant should be provided for you when returning home from a party; no strange man should constitute himself your escort. A girl so neglected would incur the risk of being treated with scant respect. It would be utterly unseemly and as much as your reputation is worth to walk out at night with any man but your father or brother. You should get home before dusk if possible, and always be accompanied by a friend if walking (even in daylight) with a man to whom you are not engaged" (1892).

This open dread of the sex-instinct served the useful purpose of protecting a girl who was compelled to earn her living by going about her business alone, but the Prudish Attitude, cultivated by years of training, was not readily abandoned, even when a certain relaxation was permitted or desirable. Thus Freda writes, in '95: "I am a clergyman's daughter. There is a young gentleman whom I am very fond of and he is exceedingly nice to me. I do not know how it is but when we see each other to speak to he and myself are awfully proper. I know it is not his shyness, for I have seen him quite jolly with other girls. I do not want to flirt with him but only to be more friendly. Can you suggest a way by which we may know each other better?" In fact, Prudery had made her too good to be true.

It was an essential feature of the Prude that while ever on the look-out for symptoms of the instinct in others, she was overcome with shame on detecting its promptings in herself. Such a one writes: "When a woman is in the humiliating position of loving a man who does not return her love, what is the best thing to do? Can I do anything to win his love without being unmaidenly? I am not at all beautiful, in fact very plain and reserved; I must do something, however small, as my life's happiness is at stake."

The urge to pry into other people's lives and detect their transgressions naturally induces in the Prude a sense of her moral superiority, but this she does not so much proclaim aloud as by implication. Sometimes the itch to "peep" is satisfied by a kind of proxy, such as a craving to thrust improving works into the hands of strangers, in the hope they may be evil-doers. Dorothy, for instance, is advised that if she wishes to do good, "we suggest you procure packets of nice little books and the Holy Gospels —each in separate form—and when you travel you can thrust them under the seat-cushion; for remember, many of the lower orders feel insulted by the offer of one, a result of which you should beware so as not to defeat your own object." Her object being, clearly, to peep by proxy and catch the sinners in the act.

There was much in the '90s to stimulate the Prudery of those addicted to that Attitude; the papers glowing with descriptions of the New Woman and her dreadful behaviour; the Fin de Siècle literature and its shocking implications of Free Love; and, of course, the New Art, with its disclosures of the obscene. And when, as the century drew to its close, the more sensual fashions of women's dress appeared, the Prude discovered a new field for investigation.

The novels and plays had been terrible in their revelations of Sex; and now shop windows displayed, in the full glare of day so that any man could inspect them, the most intimate details of Woman's toilet. Your face scorched at the things hung up—and men smiling at their bifurcations. And things were reaching a pretty pass when Undies became a nickname for Sacred Mysteries.

Even the posters were shameless; we read, in '99, a Prude's lament: "The penny weeklies contain on every page some would-be jest at the expense of maidenhood. The modern heroine is now a composition creature, loving, maybe, but calculating how to attract. . . . The same spirit of exposure stares from the hoardings; not to speak of the skimpily attired folk who illustrate the comic drama, what unveiling of the mysteries of the boudoir are placarded everywhere in the form of advertisements! A patent soap or corn-extracter cannot be commended unless Tom, Dick and Harry are invited to see a young lady in her nightgown manipulating her toes! This, methinks, is too much, and cheapens the sacredness of womanhood" . . . . One detects the workings of the prudish mind and the inevitable sequence of associated thoughts: young lady—nightgown—adultery; and in the presence of Tom and Dick and Harry the subconscious "this, methinks, is a little too much."

The Prude's Progress in the '90s

The '90s were rich in novels written in this vein by women who foamed with lucrative indignation at what they conceived to be those naughty 'Nineties, but it seems that the chief vice of that age was Prudery.

In the more educated this Attitude was necessarily more masked, so much so that in many it was wholly unconscious. The opening years of the decade carried on the Sentimentalism which had been developing at the end of the '80s but with an increased emphasis, guarded always by a sense of Fear. Infinite precautions were needed lest in a world whose barriers had been thrown down Sentiment should lead to a lowering of the moral tone. Intensity of feelings were happily deflected along innocent paths, and the banner of Purity waved over every home. This attitude seems to have inspired an inordinate love of White Paint, ever a symbol of the blameless life, and the House became a mirror of the Mind. It was painted inside and out with this refreshing colour. Your drawing-room, we read, should have "a wallpaper of delicate blue-grey; the furniture of white enamelled wood, and the over-mantel painted ivory, on which should stand a piece of Satsuma or Benares ware. Light curtains to drape the windows; carpet with camel ground and tints of grey-blue, gold and terra-cotta. Touches of terra-cotta here and there and plenty of lovely palms, ferns and aspidistras; such a room ·is within the powers of ordinary mortals to possess."

The bright wholesome effect is sustained by "lamps of all sorts and sizes, such as a pale pink lamp-shade covered with a frou-frou of white lace and clusters of apple-blossom." The air of pinkiness and prettiness would relieve the white paint of coldness without in any way suggesting that it was other than perfectly Pure.

And there must be no Dark Corners (where dust and Impurity might lurk), while on the wall an engraving of "The Hopeless Dawn" would illustrate Woman's view of the '90s.

The Fashions in Dress, obeying the impulse which had started towards the end of the previous decade, developed a curious resemblance to the sequence seen in the '20s; a growing elaboration of the upper half, with expansion of the shoulder line and upper half of the sleeve, until in '93 a full-grown "leg-of-mutton" provided a feast for the eye. At the same time vandyking above the hem, pointed waists and angular sloping lines from the shoulders carried out the superficial resemblance—but with a fundamental difference.

The emotional impulse was restrained by Fear, and Prudery aped Romance.

The huge sleeve, instead of suggesting a rapturous exuberance, was hard and formal, and the habit of making it of different material from the rest of the bodice, with a heavier tone, served to distract the eye from more intimate regions. Massive revers, perhaps of dark velvet, drew obliterating lines over the figure, or the blouse with its evasive puffing helped to disguise the indiscretions of anatomy.

The skirt underwent important changes. Modern conditions required a less hampering structure, but propriety necessitated that there should be no revelations. These requirements were beautifully met by a gored skirt. "Walking skirts are now of a sensible length and width, being 3½ yards wide and only reaching to the ankles or even a little above" (1890). Presently the five or seven gored skirt became adaptable to all occasions, varying merely in width and length. But we are warned "though skirts are narrow they must not cling," and this was prevented by stiff linings. In such a skirt a woman could walk, play tennis and golf without destroying the monolithic illusion of her sub-structure.

It was, in fact, Woman's first attempt towards

287

devising a costume for practical use that was not primarily intended to be sex-attractive. For now a large part of her time and thoughts were occupied in other matters. Yet such a uniform could be made "smart" by appropriate decoration, for the idea of smartness is often not to attract but to give an air of competence.

However, in the '90s the prime function of Woman's dress was far from forgotten, in spite of any nervous apprehensions as to the effect of its charm on Man. It was difficult for the Prude to sustain that guarded Attitude "if" (as a lady's magazine of 1890 expressed it) "Woman is to be that soft, sweet, and tender bit of humanity which Heaven distinctly intended her to be"—like a chop, not overdone. She is even bidden to attend to "the petticoat, foamingly soft, adored by man; while the clinging folds and soft outlines of the Tea Gown add a subtle attraction and dignity, varying and dangerous, and treble the fascinations of her slender Form. Moralists affirm that it must bring in its train all sorts of immoralities, but beauty-lovers of the day laugh at such absurdities. In a Tea Gown a woman will appear just 'adorable' and what more can a woman want to be?"

In outdoor costume a characteristic feature

was the Toque which symbolised the sweet purity of a flower garden; for example, "a delightful confection of green velvet with a piece of white lace falling over the brim on one side; the crown of turquoises and emeralds; and the other side a mass of violets, forget-me-nots and waving white plumes of paradise; this indeed, realises one's dream of a lovely Toque." Moreover, "Cloaks are most graceful and the frills over the shoulders are often weighted by heavy fringe, very becoming; the yokes of embroidery or velvet with the Tudor collars figure on most of them."

In order to maintain the requisite smallness of the waist it was very helpful to use the Patent Coraline Corset, guaranteed to be absolutely unbreakable under the severest strain, and to convey the impression of a "presence" the skirt should have a silk foundation that would rustle with every movement. Unfortunately a cheap substitute at a mere 2s. 6d. a yard was soon invented, which would make as much noise, and only the feminine ear could distinguish between them.

The general effect of such a costume was to impart to the wearer a "noli me tangere" air, which no doubt was very efficacious, but it was disappointing that the result did not receive the approval of contemporary artists. Mr. G. F. Watts, in 1890, was of the opinion that "the indifference in modern times to grace and harmony in dress is a strong reason for concluding that pleasure in what is beautiful is extinct"; while Mr. John Collier frankly declared that "thanks to high heels the modern female foot is a hideous object; a thing to be shuddered at."

Probably they failed to understand that high heels are not meant to add to a Woman's beauty, but only to her stature; for the Woman of the '90s was willing to compress her feet into spatulate lumps if thereby she could come up to Man's level, and her sense of Beauty was distracted by two opposite desires, the desire to attract, and the desire to rise superior to that desire.

This paradoxical Attitude produced an odd mixture of freedom and restraint in her conduct; it was possible to go where she chose by day, but the moment dusk approached she must not be seen out of doors except under protection, for it was well understood that sin and sunset come together; that she could be "a vigorous and athletic young woman who goes in for all kinds of sports in which her brothers take part"—and

yet blush for shame if by a slip she used the word
"nightdress" in a man's hearing. A still more terrible *faux pas* was committed by a girl who accidentally spoke of "a miscarriage of justice." "My
dear!" whispered her horrified mother, "Never
use such a dreadful word! Don't you know it has
—another meaning?"

It was not surprising, therefore, that some contemporaries only saw one aspect of this complex
young woman of the '90s. Thus, a very com-
petent woman of that day writes: "Girls now
have a full fine life opening before them and the
widening of the prospect is occasionally dazzling.
The girl of to-day, with her fine physical development, her bright cheery nature and her robust
contempt for all things small and mean, is an
immense improvement on the girl of yesterday.
She has a vigorous contempt for all forms of softness; her mind and character are strung up to
a firmness of which a sentimental heroine of fifty
years ago would have been ashamed. She is a
good comrade with her brothers, sharing in most
of their sports and pastimes. Her chief accomplishments are waltzing and tennis. She has her
faults; she is undoubtedly hard-hearted."

And this was a young woman laced into nineteen inches of corset, who shuddered at anything

suggestive of "sex"; who shrank from being alone with a "strange man," and hastily covered her ankles when one of the dreaded sex approached.

And when bicycling offered the possibilities of enlarging her horizon, she was torn between the desire to enjoy them and the fear lest bits of her anatomy might be exposed to passers-by. "Is it proper," one asks, "for a girl to ride a bicycle to church?"—an insoluble conundrum. But on week-days she would take the plunge in the plus-fours of an elephant, to the horror of those who felt that the Upward Movement in women's clothing had now reached the knee—plus ultra. Another, in more modest fashion, assumed a hybrid garment, becoming an ambiguous biped who used her legs but denied their existence. "The simplest and best costume" (a contemporary writes) "consists of warm combinations, a thick woollen vest or knitted bodice, and a pair of tweed or cloth knickerbockers, with a skirt of water-proofed cloth made closely fitting and rather long in front so as not to display a too liberal allowance of ankle, with a Norfolk jacket and small felt hat. Thus equipped the rider can brave any kind of weather and need not be afraid of accident."

But there were other accidents besides the

weather. In an article in '97 one of "the old school" laments this modern bicycling craze; not only is it far beyond a girl's strength, "but it tends to destroy the sweet simplicity of her girlish nature; besides, how dreadful it would be if, by some accident, she were to fall off into the arms of a strange man!"

The phrase expresses, in a nutshell, the feminine psychology of the '90s; the eternal fear of falling into the arms of a strange man; modern psychologists have taught us that a persistent Fear is, in reality, a disguised Wish.

That this latent Fear—or disguised Wish— was ever present in Women's minds, is revealed by a study of the popular magazines, which at that period supplied such an important food for their starving instinct. If the plots of the short stories contained in them are analysed, it will be seen that an enormous proportion of them can be reduced to the formula "falling into the arms of a strange man." And this is always presented as being an agreeable process, for however the crude plot may be dressed up with picturesque details it has a constant feature; the Strange Man proves to be a Good Young Man, heavily charged with Self-restraint; consequently the adventure of falling into his arms leads to nothing more alarming than marriage. Those were the days of the Clean-limbed Young Englishman, ever ready to Take Up the White Man's Burden in the shape of a blushing bride whom he would carry off to the altar. Or more precisely, those were the days when that engaging young man abounded—in magazines. To heighten the thrill for the reader the author might devise circumstances in which two complete strangers (of opposite sexes) were forced into conversation without being introduced—a wreck or a railway accident such as might happen any day to you, dear reader—and then the heroine would experience the delicious embarrassment of being actually accosted by a Strange Man. We read of a girl, quite a nice girl without an atom of *arrière-pensée,* who falls overboard, whereupon He leaps to the rescue, and while respectfully supporting her with one hand (as the illustration in half-tone clearly indicates) he takes off his hat with the other and asks her to be his wife. Thrilled by being alone in the Atlantic with a Strange Man, she murmurs a watery "Yes.". . .

Or the position may be reversed, as with the heroine who, in maidenly meditation, perceives over the edge of the cliff a young man stuck halfway up, unable to move. As a substitute for a rope she tears strips off her petticoat and, blushing deeply, uses them to drag him to safety. When he recognises the means by which his life has been saved he behaves like a gentleman and proposes, while she is overcome by the ravishing thought that a Strange Man had been handling portions of her underclothing.

One cannot but notice that in the stories of this period the Strange Man never turns out to be a villain; indeed, the black character, if there is one, is a Villainess; the inference is clear; any Strange Man is a desirable object and any other female is a potential rival, and therefore a bad woman. Sometimes, of course, He has faults, such as smoking to excess, but these are of a kind which marriage would cure.

These magazines, if examined from another aspect, supply a very suggestive sign. They abound in Baby-Worship, with masses of stories and pictures of children, young animals and little birds. The proportion of this kind of matter far exceeds the normal, and indicates an insatiable appetite, and was, no doubt, very comforting to a starved instinct.

Sometimes the more urgent craving to be pursued by the monster, Man, is gratified in symbolic form, the heroine being chased by a ferocious animal, such as a lion, or even the prosaic bull, and rescued in the nick of time by Purity clothed in a Norfolk jacket and knickerbockers, scented deliciously with tobacco. It is a kind of allegory dear to the feminine mind, but especially to the hungry maiden of the '90s.

Those magazines are far more valuable than the great novels, because they reveal, when properly translated, the subconscious thoughts of their readers, but even the novels of the '90s are not without merit. The wish to discover some redeeming charm in the blackest of villains, and in the Sorrows of Satan himself a theme for feminine pity, indicates a desire to remove that dread of the Male.

But the perpetual harping on this theme shows how widespread that Fear must have been. It had its redeeming features, for as an emotional stimulus it must have supplied constant small thrills to the virgin mind. When the display of a few inches of petticoat would always provoke an immediate reaction in Man, it was impossible to deny that sex-attraction was in the reach of the plainest, but she felt she was playing with fire. So the Prude turned to the magazines to give what she dared not take from real life.

The Prude's Progress in the '90s

In that rapidly modernising world it was natural that the Gothic Attitude of mind, with its decorative concealments of the obvious and persistent evasion of facts, should arouse in a minority of contemporaries a fierce scorn and contempt.

To them it seemed an urgent necessity that faded and futile conventions should be stripped off, and reality exposed "in all its naked hideousness." A band of enthusiasts therefore arose, inspired by the principles of Exhibitionism, and proceeded by conduct and appearance and works of Art to *épater le bourgeois*. She who aped the masculine in dress and manners was nick-named The New Woman, and provoked an extraordinary outburst of fury. "The New Woman is neither a Lady nor a Gentleman," was the popular cry. It is characteristic that whenever the nation leans strongly towards the Sentimental Attitude, it regards Exhibitionism and its by-product, Perversion, with special horror, and so in the '90s the New Woman seemed a portent of evil. Then, suddenly, by an ironic stroke of Fate, the subject was forced into public recognition by a notorious trial. The purest of the pure-minded could not open a newspaper without having the nameless horror thrust under their

very nose. The psychological effect was to produce a strong counter-movement towards Sentimentalism.

Another aspect of the Exhibitionism of the
early '90s was shown in the literature of that
period; for the first time the relationships of men
and women were depicted in realistic fashion.
"Fin de Siècle literature is the cult of glare, the
apotheosis of the 'nothing concealed'; by another
name it is Realism, the analysis of the Unclean,
the deification of the Dirty" (1890). Such was
the opinion of the majority, who, without denying
the existence of the Unclean, saw no advantage
in public washing. Women writers began to
analyse married life, and the new novels began
where the old used to end. Secrets of the alcove
were dragged into light; some writers seemed to
advocate a degree of licence for which respectable folk could not discover a respectable name;
and when at length an author, hitherto of blameless reputation, held up for admiration the
portrait of a Woman Who Did, it seemed that Fin
de Siècle was synonymous with Fin du Monde.
The whole basis of Victorian family ethics was
disputed; was Woman entitled to regard the instincts of sex as though they were mere physical
faculties to be utilised at her own pleasure, when

Authority had definitely pronounced them to be
a moral incubus?

The crude attempts at Naturalism in the
novels of the '90s were startling innovations;
hitherto no real effort had been made by English
writers to penetrate deeper than the surface of
the feminine mind. If, for example, one examines
the novels in which the most intimate relationship between man and woman is depicted, the
Woman's Attitude is always portrayed as it
would have been seen by a man, or else as it
would have been seen by the conventional world;
it lacks the peculiar feminine flavour. There have
been hosts of novels in which seduction of the
heroine forms the dramatic crisis; one recalls the
figures of Effie Dean, Little Em'ly, Hettie Sorrel,
Tess of the D'Urbervilles, and Esther Waters,
stretching from one end of the century to the
other; but it was not until Tess appeared in the
'80s that any attempt was made by the author
to develop the woman's character after the crisis
in her life. Formerly the literary convention was
that she should immediately become static, a
wooden image of remorse and despair, seen
objectively. In Tess, the author tried to go
further and display the mental changes following
her physical catastrophe, but, in fact, gave little

more than a picture of the results; we do not feel her experiences, we only witness them. George Moore presented his study of the theme as a thesis to show that such an experience may lead to the drying-up of the passionate instinct, as a barrister might demonstrate the feelings of his client. There was no English novel in the 19th century portraying the perpetual workings of sex-instinct on Woman as she herself would view it in moments of self-analysis. Such would, doubtless, have been regarded as highly indelicate.

Similarly there was no *intrinsic* analysis of the maternal feelings, or of the psychological effects of the death of husband or child on the feminine mind, but only immobilised figures.

In fact, the 19th century novel tells us very little of psychological value, except by some chance slip of the pen, and we have to apply modern psycho-analytical methods in order to understand the 19th century woman. The novelist may have been an artist, but he was entirely under the influence of the Gothic tradition, which aims at graceful concealment rather than precise truth. His heroine was permitted to have a heart-ache but never a stomach-ache, and yet one must suppose that the claims of the

body occasionally assailed even a Victorian
heroine.

We hardly know how she spoke in real life, for
literary convention required a language of its own
which, to the modern ear, seems to conceal just
what we most want to hear. Those heroines of
Scott, Dickens, Thackeray, George Eliot,
Meredith and the rest, what did they blurt out
when the audience was not there? What did they
think of the restrictions, mental and physical?
what—especially—did they really think of the
Man of their day?

Had the young woman in their pages any intelligent anticipations, any apprehensions? And
what did disillusionment feel like? Was the great
Maternity Stunt agreeable to their mid-Victorian
tastes? We are simply not told.

It is easy to understand why the Realistic
School of writers of the '90s provoked so much
alarm; it almost looked as though, in another
moment, they might let out the truth; but they
were more concerned to blurt out the Unmention-
ables which have no great significance, instead of
the Mentionables which appear everywhere
except in novels. They exposed, but they did not
explain. For the Exhibitionist is no more capable
of explaining life than the Sentimentalist.

The battle between them raged furiously in those Fin de Siècle days, and the discussion of facts which everyone knew but no one mentioned was now carried a stage further by dramatists, who depicted the lives of women who had declined the protection of marriage; of people whose moral irregularities were analysed before a mixed audience on a stage set to resemble a bedroom. . . .

More popular places of entertainment displayed Living Pictures of young women in pink flesh tights posing as La Source . . . and there were places where one could see the Victorian Age on its last legs, displaying acres of underclothing in one long last lingering High Kick. . . .

Such revelations of Body and Mind were very disturbing to the average Woman of the '90s; they seemed to destroy the Great Illusion, and to offer no effective substitute. Nor was the fault by any means one-sided. "It is a pity men and women say such ungracious things about one another. To-day it is the woman who is the aggressor. In fiction, essays and on platforms they are employing their newly developed powers in proving what a poor creature Man is. It is evident to every observer of current events that the whole question of marriage is passing through a period of severe criticism" (1896).

It may be noted that the marriage rate had fallen to fifteen per thousand, and the marriage age of women had risen to 24½; of every thousand brides, whereas the proportion of those under age had risen rapidly from 1847 to 1857 (from 143 to 223 per 1000), after that date it had declined and was, at the end of the century, back again to the level of 1850 (namely at 170 per 1000).

Owing to economic conditions and the discovery of alternative careers, a large number of women had already established a move to abolish the stigma of being unmarried; indeed the single state was advocated as one of moral and intellectual superiority. We are told in '92 that "the Bachelor Girl is a distinct product of the last decade; she sets up either by herself or in partnership with one of her own sex." There was, in fact, a growing inclination to criticise the conventional Attitude towards the natural instincts. All sorts of provisional solutions were suggested, experimented with, and abandoned. The *moral* quality which hung over the whole subject like a cloud seemed to prevent any clarity of vision. Some enthusiasts would denounce at the tops of their voices its very existence; but "methinks the lady doth protest too much"; others declared that the cultivation of the Abnormal was the only cure for the Normal, while the vast majority shrank from the subject, and, hugging their chains, maintained that there was no problem at all.

Yet looking back at these various Attitudes it is not difficult for us to see that beneath "all the desires for freedom, experience, pleasure, love, change and movement—all the newly awakened thoughts and aspirations of this restless age" (as a writer in '90 described it), there lay the insoluble problem, how is a modern State to manage an ancient instinct so that it can find adequate expression without distortion or stunting? Is it a problem of theology, or morals, or psychology, or merely hygiene? It seems that the greater part of the '90s was preoccupied with suggesting solutions without having first determined the answer to that question.

Towards the close of the century the wrangle died down. Woman decided that after all it pays best to be charming.

We find, about '98, a radical change in the fashion of her dress. The ungainly bulk of the sleeves vanished. "They appear to grow tighter and smaller and longer every week." And presently the bodice displayed the shape of

Nature. Even early in the decade we had been told that "none of the once popular 'bust improvers' of wire, air cushions or coiled hair are tolerated now. The woman with no bust at all is the modiste's delight for she is convinced that not even the Creator can design such delightful curves and graceful slopes as she can produce with her wadding and whalebone." The art of perfecting imperfections was, by the end of the century, superlatively successful. "The event of the past year," it was said in '99, "is the return of the figure; the seamless skirt, the tightly swathed bodice and glovelike sleeve, and the longer-waisted rigid stays, and soft unstarched petticoats; the skirt, tightly fitting round the hips, is made on the circular form; with a tight-fitting coat and skirt the woman of fashion may look a miracle of curves and grace."

In a word, after years of indecision, Woman had resumed her Curves, and the joyful news was proclaimed by undulations from top to toe. It was the Attitude in which she determined to face the new century. We, who are no longer subjected to that form of allurement, may, perhaps, admire without adoration the success of the picture she presented. The new device of building the skirt from segments of a circle gave it a novel effect, the "flare." The sinuous line descending from those dominating hips, the appealing femininity of the bodice, the picture hat balanced and skewered on a coiffure of waves and puffs and pads, gave her an air of absolute assurance, as she moved with that provocative pelvic roll . . . perhaps the most sensual Attitude of the century. It was a calculated pose, and had a curious resemblance to that of 1830.

Was this, then, to be the conclusion of the whole matter, a frank return to the orchidaceous?

But she could survey the past century with a good deal of satisfaction; favours, privileges, rights, she had wrung them all from her ancient foe, and now, armed with new weapons and still possessed of the old, she could, in the new century perhaps, win fresh victories over him.

Yet in those solitary moments when the feminine mind is prone suddenly to lose courage, and to long for objective support, the cold shadow of a doubt would arise. She had used her Instincts to civilise Man; was she capable, now, of civilising herself?

"And whether, stepping forth, my soul shall
see
New wonders, or fall sheer, a blinded
thing. . . ."

ADVERTISEMENTS

1806

This day is published PATHETIC, SENTIMENTAL,
& MORAL NARRATIVES in twelve Monthly numbers,
each embellished with highly finished Engraving. Price
1/-. Each number to contain several complete stories.
Every attention will be paid to the strictest principles
of Morality & Virtue; whatever may in the most trifling
degree militate against those principles, tend to mislead
the judgment or inflame the imagination, will be carefully rejected; Information will be united with Pleasure;
& Virtue, although in distress, will preserve her native
loveliness & dignity. To excite the pure tear of sensibility,
to foster the best feelings of humanity & to amend the
heart, will be the unvaried attempts of the Editor.

1807   LADIES

The delicate & restrained condition which custom im-
poses on females subjects them to great disadvantages.
Mrs. Morris offers to remove them. Ladies or Gentlemen
who have formed predilections may be assisted in obtain-
ing the objects of their affections; & those who are un-
engaged may be immediately introduced to suitable persons; but she cannot assist applicants in any marriage
if their characters are not irreproachable, & their fortunes
considerable & independent. She will not admit any others.
Apply at the bow-window next to Margaret Chapel,
Cavendish Square. Ladies who require it may be waited
on at their own houses.

1808

SEMINARY FOR YOUNG LADIES, ALBION HOUSE, EPSOM

The Public are respectfully informed that the above Establishment is now wholly superintended by Mrs. Riley. Her terms for the education of young Ladies are as follow:—

For the English & French Languages grammatically, Astronomy, Geography, the use of the Globes, projection of the Sphere, History, ancient & modern, & Needlework, Thirty-five Guineas per annum; no entrance. Writing, Geometry, Drawing, Music, Singing & Dancing, taught by Masters of eminence on approved terms. Mrs. Riley dispenses with the usual technical routine of promises & professions, convinced that to those acquainted with her course & stile of instruction, such is not necessary, & to those who are not, egotism ought not to recommend her; upon the opinion of her friends & the consciousness of her Pupils, therefore, she rests her claims as a Preceptress of youth.

1809   BEAUTY ANIMATED & VISION PRESERVED

A healthy pellucid eye is the prime messenger of intellect, the immediate herald of the soul; it conveys our sentiments & our passions with the rapidity of the solar ray, forming an aetherial language almost superseding the faculty of speech; hence its persuasive effect in colloquial intercourse, in the consolatory effusions of friendship, & the coruscations of amatory eloquence.

The *Kollurion* or *Grecian Eye Water* gives tone & lustre to the healthy Eye, in Inflammation unrivalled, & so safe that it may be applied to the most tender subject; & is the peculiar friend of Sea-bathers by washing off the saline

particles. This balmy fluid has the solicitude of a
Physician of distinguished talent; is prepared by him &
sold only by Messrs. Price & Co. in bottles at 10/6 each.
A letter, post-paid, with a pound note, will command
two bottles to any part of the kingdom.

1824

Those of our fair countrywomen who have not hitherto
resorted to the KALYDOR as a never-failing specific
for all cutaneous deformities, including freckles, pimples,
spots, redness, & every other imperfection incident to the
skin, it will be found on trial that this invaluable cosmetic
is the most powerful protector in the universe of female
beauty against the inclemencies of weather, change of
climate, & aggression of disease, & with the stability of
eternal friendship, that it will sustain the mighty powers
of female attraction to the latest period of human
existence.

1838

Mrs. Nicholas Geary, Stay and Corset Maker to Her
Majesty Queen Adelaide, offers to the notice of the
Female world her New Invented Anatomical Stay, devised
upon such scientific principles as to entirely exclude all
that injurious pressure which prevails in all other Stays,
at the same time producing a figure of such exquisite
symmetry that attempted in any other Stay would almost
amount to suffocation.

1838   FOR THE HAIR

Patronised by Her most Gracious Majesty & used by
thousands whose testimonials convince the most sceptical

of the efficacy of *Dawson's Auxiliary* to restore hair from baldness or greyness, however extreme, & entirely remove dandriffe. It produces eyebrows & whiskers, & beautiful hair on children's heads.

1840

AN APPEAL FOR FUNDS FOR BUILDING A NATIONAL SCHOOL AT WOODSTOCK

An humble individual ventures to appeal in a cause dear to every English heart—the maintenance of good order & right principles among the Poor. The Rector requires £100 more to build the school & rescue the youthful members of his flock from demoralising idleness. You who are Mothers—give them respectability in this life, & the hope of happiness in another!

1847

To the Nobility and Gentry. Tiffin & Son, BUG-DESTROYERS to the Royal Family, beg to suggest the propriety of having this nuisance removed. When it is understood this business has been conducted with respectability, success, & despatch above 150 years amongst the first circles it will scarcely require further recommendation.

1847   5TH EDITION OF "ADVICE TO THE MILLION"

contains the Ladies' Pudding, which will remove constipation & infuse the strength of the horse into the constitution, with the Rules for Rising refreshed after sleep, at any hour in the morning, without being awoke. Also, how to enjoy something at home in the winter, which may be had almost without expense; with the secret of having a fresh set of undergarments daily without any additional cost, showing how individuals of limited means may become capitalists. May be had by enclosing eight penny stamps.

1847

Beautiful Women. The Thorn that veils the Primrose from our view is not more invidious in Nature than superfluous hair on face, neck & arms of beauty. For its removal HUBERT'S ROSEATE POWDER stands pre-eminent.

1847

Important to Ladies wishing to preserve the Hair of a Relative or Friend. Mr. DEWNEY wishes to state that he is a WORKING ARTIST & that hair entrusted to him does not leave his possession until made & returned in the form desired. An elegant Hair & Gold Ring 3/6; fine guard ditto 5/6.

1847

New Monthly Work, to be completed in six parts, price 1/- each, by a Lady who has gone through a great deal; dedicated to the Wives & Mothers of England.

THE GREATEST PLAGUE IN LIFE; or the Adventures of a Lady in search of a good servant. By one who has been nearly worried to death. This work the Lady is induced to publish from motives of benevolence rather than gain, deeming that the troubles she has undergone, & the restless nights she has passed, together with the distress she has endured might be interesting as well as instructive to those young wives who are entering upon the thorny path of married life. The Lady is happy to have it in her power to state that that delightful artist, Mr. George Cruikshank, has in the most gentlemanly way consented to embellish the work with Portraits of the principal of the ungrateful creatures who have successively converted her happy fireside into (if she may be allowed the expression) a "maison de deuil." It is but right to add that the Lady is herself both a wife & the Mother of a large family.

1847

In two elegant Vols., royal quarto, bound in cloth £5; in morocco, £7.7. the Marriage Day Present BIBLE, illustrated with 180 highly finished Engravings.

1849

The Registered Bust Improver. For the purpose of aiding the Dress & Stay-maker in giving an elegant figure & appearance to the wearer. Up to the present time pads made of Cotton and Wool have been much used for improving the Bust; to do away with the evident defects of these this invention claims the attention of all parties interested in the use of it. The advantages to be obtained by it are gracefulness of Development, a perfect fit of the Dress, & ease & comfort in the Wear. This article is manufactured of an air-proof material & sold in boxes of half a dozen by J. White, of Gresham St.

1849   CORSETS—STAYS—CORSETS !!

George Roberts, after 20 years' experience, having discovered the art of supplying the Public with three pairs of this indispensable article at the price usually charged for one pair, most respectfully solicits Ladies of nobility & gentry to an inspection of his 100 patterns. Prices for 18 inches, 13/- rising -/6 an inch.

Crinoline & Moreen slips & Bustles in endless variety.

1852   HEARTS UNITED

Hair Rings, & lined throughout with good solid gold, & two gold hearts united upon, with the Initials........5/6.

The same, with two gold hands united in place of hearts 7/6

1867   2000 SANSFLECTUM & EBONITE CRINOLINES,

warranted not to melt with the heat of the fire, & will not rust with the water, & are adapted for winter & seaside wear. Patronised by ROYALTY.

N.B. The Patent EBONITE SKIRT, with scarlet or violet flounce from 20/- upwards.

1876

The 28 guinea INCOMPARABLE Dining-room Suite, in solid Ash, pure Mediæval style, & superior manufacture, includes all the entire Furniture for a Dining-room, with full-sized sideboard, waggon, etc. & chairs in best leather, is especially recommended to clergymen & others, & considered to be the greatest speciality yet introduced for economy & character.

1881   THIN BUSTS

Ideal Corset for perfecting thin figures. Words cannot describe its charming effect, which is unapproachable & unattainable by any other Corset in the World. Softly padded Regulators inside (with other improvements combining softness, lightness & comfort) regulate at wearer's pleasure any desired fullness with the graceful curves of a beautifully proportioned bust. As guarantee of genuineness a single Corset sent on approval in plain parcel on receipt of remittance. Money returned if desired. Avoid worthless substitutes.

1897   LATEST NOVELTY

The PNEUMATIC TUBE COIL is to all appearance an ordinary switch of hair, but hidden away in the centre is a pliable tube of hair & thinnest wire, so that when coiled the appearance is that of thickness without the weight that results from a great quantity of hair. It cannot get ruffled, or out of order, even with the pressure of a hat or bonnet. Price from £2.10. New Pompadour Toupee £3.3 to £4.4.

Cycle & Seaside Fringe 10/6. Transformation on hairnet foundation, with side parting 5 guineas.

1897

HAIR permanently destroyed & BLUSHING permanently cured by simple & harmless Home treatment.

A CATALOG OF SELECTED DOVER
BOOKS IN ALL FIELDS OF INTEREST

CONCERNING THE SPIRITUAL IN ART, Wassily Kandinsky. Pioneering work by father of abstract art. Thoughts on color theory, nature of art. Analysis of earlier masters. 12 illustrations. 80pp. of text. 5⅜ x 8½. 23411-8

ANIMALS: 1,419 Copyright-Free Illustrations of Mammals, Birds, Fish, Insects, etc., Jim Harter (ed.). Clear wood engravings present, in extremely lifelike poses, over 1,000 species of animals. One of the most extensive pictorial sourcebooks of its kind. Captions. Index. 284pp. 9 x 12. 23766-4

CELTIC ART: The Methods of Construction, George Bain. Simple geometric techniques for making Celtic interlacements, spirals, Kells-type initials, animals, humans, etc. Over 500 illustrations. 160pp. 9 x 12. (Available in U.S. only.) 22923-8

AN ATLAS OF ANATOMY FOR ARTISTS, Fritz Schider. Most thorough reference work on art anatomy in the world. Hundreds of illustrations, including selections from works by Vesalius, Leonardo, Goya, Ingres, Michelangelo, others. 593 illustrations. 192pp. 7⅛ x 10¼. 20241-0

CELTIC HAND STROKE-BY-STROKE (Irish Half-Uncial from "The Book of Kells"): An Arthur Baker Calligraphy Manual, Arthur Baker. Complete guide to creating each letter of the alphabet in distinctive Celtic manner. Covers hand position, strokes, pens, inks, paper, more. Illustrated. 48pp. 8¼ x 11. 24336-2

EASY ORIGAMI, John Montroll. Charming collection of 32 projects (hat, cup, pelican, piano, swan, many more) specially designed for the novice origami hobbyist. Clearly illustrated easy-to-follow instructions insure that even beginning papercrafters will achieve successful results. 48pp. 8¼ x 11. 27298-2

THE COMPLETE BOOK OF BIRDHOUSE CONSTRUCTION FOR WOODWORKERS, Scott D. Campbell. Detailed instructions, illustrations, tables. Also data on bird habitat and instinct patterns. Bibliography. 3 tables. 63 illustrations in 15 figures. 48pp. 5¼ x 8½. 24407-5

BLOOMINGDALE'S ILLUSTRATED 1886 CATALOG: Fashions, Dry Goods and Housewares, Bloomingdale Brothers. Famed merchants' extremely rare catalog depicting about 1,700 products: clothing, housewares, firearms, dry goods, jewelry, more. Invaluable for dating, identifying vintage items. Also, copyright-free graphics for artists, designers. Co-published with Henry Ford Museum & Greenfield Village. 160pp. 8¼ x 11. 25780-0

HISTORIC COSTUME IN PICTURES, Braun & Schneider. Over 1,450 costumed figures in clearly detailed engravings—from dawn of civilization to end of 19th century. Captions. Many folk costumes. 256pp. 8⅜ x 11¾. 23150-X

STICKLEY CRAFTSMAN FURNITURE CATALOGS, Gustav Stickley and L. & J. G. Stickley. Beautiful, functional furniture in two authentic catalogs from 1910. 594 illustrations, including 277 photos, show settles, rockers, armchairs, reclining chairs, bookcases, desks, tables. 183pp. 6½ x 9¼. 23838-5

AMERICAN LOCOMOTIVES IN HISTORIC PHOTOGRAPHS: 1858 to 1949, Ron Ziel (ed.). A rare collection of 126 meticulously detailed official photographs, called "builder portraits," of American locomotives that majestically chronicle the rise of steam locomotive power in America. Introduction. Detailed captions. xi+ 129pp. 9 x 12. 27393-8

AMERICA'S LIGHTHOUSES: An Illustrated History, Francis Ross Holland, Jr. Delightfully written, profusely illustrated fact-filled survey of over 200 American lighthouses since 1716. History, anecdotes, technological advances, more. 240pp. 8 x 10¾. 25576-X

TOWARDS A NEW ARCHITECTURE, Le Corbusier. Pioneering manifesto by founder of "International School." Technical and aesthetic theories, views of industry, economics, relation of form to function, "mass-production split" and much more. Profusely illustrated. 320pp. 6⅛ x 9¼. (Available in U.S. only.) 25023-7

HOW THE OTHER HALF LIVES, Jacob Riis. Famous journalistic record, exposing poverty and degradation of New York slums around 1900, by major social reformer. 100 striking and influential photographs. 233pp. 10 x 7⅞. 22012-5

FRUIT KEY AND TWIG KEY TO TREES AND SHRUBS, William M. Harlow. One of the handiest and most widely used identification aids. Fruit key covers 120 deciduous and evergreen species; twig key 160 deciduous species. Easily used. Over 300 photographs. 126pp. 5⅜ x 8½. 20511-8

COMMON BIRD SONGS, Dr. Donald J. Borror. Songs of 60 most common U.S. birds: robins, sparrows, cardinals, bluejays, finches, more—arranged in order of increasing complexity. Up to 9 variations of songs of each species.
Cassette and manual 99911-4

ORCHIDS AS HOUSE PLANTS, Rebecca Tyson Northen. Grow cattleyas and many other kinds of orchids—in a window, in a case, or under artificial light. 63 illustrations. 148pp. 5⅜ x 8½. 23261-1

MONSTER MAZES, Dave Phillips. Masterful mazes at four levels of difficulty. Avoid deadly perils and evil creatures to find magical treasures. Solutions for all 32 exciting illustrated puzzles. 48pp. 8¼ x 11. 26005-4

MOZART'S DON GIOVANNI (DOVER OPERA LIBRETTO SERIES), Wolfgang Amadeus Mozart. Introduced and translated by Ellen H. Bleiler. Standard Italian libretto, with complete English translation. Convenient and thoroughly portable—an ideal companion for reading along with a recording or the performance itself. Introduction. List of characters. Plot summary. 121pp. 5¼ x 8½. 24944-1

TECHNICAL MANUAL AND DICTIONARY OF CLASSICAL BALLET, Gail Grant. Defines, explains, comments on steps, movements, poses and concepts. 15-page pictorial section. Basic book for student, viewer. 127pp. 5⅜ x 8½. 21843-0

THE CLARINET AND CLARINET PLAYING, David Pino. Lively, comprehensive work features suggestions about technique, musicianship, and musical interpretation, as well as guidelines for teaching, making your own reeds, and preparing for public performance. Includes an intriguing look at clarinet history. "A godsend," *The Clarinet,* Journal of the International Clarinet Society. Appendixes. 7 illus. 320pp. 5⅜ x 8½. 40270-3

HOLLYWOOD GLAMOR PORTRAITS, John Kobal (ed.). 145 photos from 1926-49. Harlow, Gable, Bogart, Bacall; 94 stars in all. Full background on photographers, technical aspects. 160pp. 8⅜ x 11¼. 23352-9

THE ANNOTATED CASEY AT THE BAT: A Collection of Ballads about the Mighty Casey/Third, Revised Edition, Martin Gardner (ed.). Amusing sequels and parodies of one of America's best-loved poems: Casey's Revenge, Why Casey Whiffed, Casey's Sister at the Bat, others. 256pp. 5⅜ x 8½. 28598-7

THE RAVEN AND OTHER FAVORITE POEMS, Edgar Allan Poe. Over 40 of the author's most memorable poems: "The Bells," "Ulalume," "Israfel," "To Helen," "The Conqueror Worm," "Eldorado," "Annabel Lee," many more. Alphabetic lists of titles and first lines. 64pp. 5$\frac{3}{16}$ x 8¼. 26685-0

PERSONAL MEMOIRS OF U. S. GRANT, Ulysses Simpson Grant. Intelligent, deeply moving firsthand account of Civil War campaigns, considered by many the finest military memoirs ever written. Includes letters, historic photographs, maps and more. 528pp. 6⅛ x 9¼. 28587-1

ANCIENT EGYPTIAN MATERIALS AND INDUSTRIES, A. Lucas and J. Harris. Fascinating, comprehensive, thoroughly documented text describes this ancient civilization's vast resources and the processes that incorporated them in daily life, including the use of animal products, building materials, cosmetics, perfumes and incense, fibers, glazed ware, glass and its manufacture, materials used in the mummification process, and much more. 544pp. 6⅛ x 9¼. (Available in U.S. only.) 40446-3

RUSSIAN STORIES/RUSSKIE RASSKAZY: A Dual-Language Book, edited by Gleb Struve. Twelve tales by such masters as Chekhov, Tolstoy, Dostoevsky, Pushkin, others. Excellent word-for-word English translations on facing pages, plus teaching and study aids, Russian/English vocabulary, biographical/critical introductions, more. 416pp. 5⅜ x 8½. 26244-8

PHILADELPHIA THEN AND NOW: 60 Sites Photographed in the Past and Present, Kenneth Finkel and Susan Oyama. Rare photographs of City Hall, Logan Square, Independence Hall, Betsy Ross House, other landmarks juxtaposed with contemporary views. Captures changing face of historic city. Introduction. Captions. 128pp. 8¼ x 11. 25790-8

AIA ARCHITECTURAL GUIDE TO NASSAU AND SUFFOLK COUNTIES, LONG ISLAND, The American Institute of Architects, Long Island Chapter, and the Society for the Preservation of Long Island Antiquities. Comprehensive, well-researched and generously illustrated volume brings to life over three centuries of Long Island's great architectural heritage. More than 240 photographs with authoritative, extensively detailed captions. 176pp. 8¼ x 11. 26946-9

NORTH AMERICAN INDIAN LIFE: Customs and Traditions of 23 Tribes, Elsie Clews Parsons (ed.). 27 fictionalized essays by noted anthropologists examine religion, customs, government, additional facets of life among the Winnebago, Crow, Zuni, Eskimo, other tribes. 480pp. 6⅛ x 9¼. 27377-6

FRANK LLOYD WRIGHT'S DANA HOUSE, Donald Hoffmann. Pictorial essay of residential masterpiece with over 160 interior and exterior photos, plans, elevations, sketches and studies. 128pp. 9¼ x 10¾. 29120-0

THE MALE AND FEMALE FIGURE IN MOTION: 60 Classic Photographic Sequences, Eadweard Muybridge. 60 true-action photographs of men and women walking, running, climbing, bending, turning, etc., reproduced from rare 19th-century masterpiece. vi + 121pp. 9 x 12. 24745-7

1001 QUESTIONS ANSWERED ABOUT THE SEASHORE, N. J. Berrill and Jacquelyn Berrill. Queries answered about dolphins, sea snails, sponges, starfish, fishes, shore birds, many others. Covers appearance, breeding, growth, feeding, much more. 305pp. 5¼ x 8¼. 23366-9

ATTRACTING BIRDS TO YOUR YARD, William J. Weber. Easy-to-follow guide offers advice on how to attract the greatest diversity of birds: birdhouses, feeders, water and waterers, much more. 96pp. 5³⁄₁₆ x 8¼. 28927-3

MEDICINAL AND OTHER USES OF NORTH AMERICAN PLANTS: A Historical Survey with Special Reference to the Eastern Indian Tribes, Charlotte Erichsen-Brown. Chronological historical citations document 500 years of usage of plants, trees, shrubs native to eastern Canada, northeastern U.S. Also complete identifying information. 343 illustrations. 544pp. 6½ x 9¼. 25951-X

STORYBOOK MAZES, Dave Phillips. 23 stories and mazes on two-page spreads: Wizard of Oz, Treasure Island, Robin Hood, etc. Solutions. 64pp. 8¼ x 11. 23628-5

AMERICAN NEGRO SONGS: 230 Folk Songs and Spirituals, Religious and Secular, John W. Work. This authoritative study traces the African influences of songs sung and played by black Americans at work, in church, and as entertainment. The author discusses the lyric significance of such songs as "Swing Low, Sweet Chariot," "John Henry," and others and offers the words and music for 230 songs. Bibliography. Index of Song Titles. 272pp. 6½ x 9¼. 40271-1

MOVIE-STAR PORTRAITS OF THE FORTIES, John Kobal (ed.). 163 glamor, studio photos of 106 stars of the 1940s: Rita Hayworth, Ava Gardner, Marlon Brando, Clark Gable, many more. 176pp. 8⅜ x 11¼. 23546-7

BENCHLEY LOST AND FOUND, Robert Benchley. Finest humor from early 30s, about pet peeves, child psychologists, post office and others. Mostly unavailable elsewhere. 73 illustrations by Peter Arno and others. 183pp. 5⅜ x 8½. 22410-4

YEKL and THE IMPORTED BRIDEGROOM AND OTHER STORIES OF YIDDISH NEW YORK, Abraham Cahan. Film Hester Street based on *Yekl* (1896). Novel, other stories among first about Jewish immigrants on N.Y.'s East Side. 240pp. 5⅜ x 8½. 22427-9

SELECTED POEMS, Walt Whitman. Generous sampling from *Leaves of Grass*. Twenty-four poems include "I Hear America Singing," "Song of the Open Road," "I Sing the Body Electric," "When Lilacs Last in the Dooryard Bloom'd," "O Captain! My Captain!"—all reprinted from an authoritative edition. Lists of titles and first lines. 128pp. 5³⁄₁₆ x 8¼. 26878-0

CATALOG OF DOVER BOOKS

THE BEST TALES OF HOFFMANN, E. T. A. Hoffmann. 10 of Hoffmann's most important stories: "Nutcracker and the King of Mice," "The Golden Flowerpot," etc. 458pp. 5⅜ x 8½. 21793-0

FROM FETISH TO GOD IN ANCIENT EGYPT, E. A. Wallis Budge. Rich detailed survey of Egyptian conception of "God" and gods, magic, cult of animals, Osiris, more. Also, superb English translations of hymns and legends. 240 illustrations. 545pp. 5⅜ x 8½. 25803-3

FRENCH STORIES/CONTES FRANÇAIS: A Dual-Language Book, Wallace Fowlie. Ten stories by French masters, Voltaire to Camus: "Micromegas" by Voltaire; "The Atheist's Mass" by Balzac; "Minuet" by de Maupassant; "The Guest" by Camus, six more. Excellent English translations on facing pages. Also French-English vocabulary list, exercises, more. 352pp. 5⅜ x 8½. 26443-2

CHICAGO AT THE TURN OF THE CENTURY IN PHOTOGRAPHS: 122 Historic Views from the Collections of the Chicago Historical Society, Larry A. Viskochil. Rare large-format prints offer detailed views of City Hall, State Street, the Loop, Hull House, Union Station, many other landmarks, circa 1904-1913. Introduction. Captions. Maps. 144pp. 9⅜ x 12¼. 24656-6

OLD BROOKLYN IN EARLY PHOTOGRAPHS, 1865-1929, William Lee Younger. Luna Park, Gravesend race track, construction of Grand Army Plaza, moving of Hotel Brighton, etc. 157 previously unpublished photographs. 165pp. 8⅞ x 11¾. 23587-4

THE MYTHS OF THE NORTH AMERICAN INDIANS, Lewis Spence. Rich anthology of the myths and legends of the Algonquins, Iroquois, Pawnees and Sioux, prefaced by an extensive historical and ethnological commentary. 36 illustrations. 480pp. 5⅜ x 8½. 25967-6

AN ENCYCLOPEDIA OF BATTLES: Accounts of Over 1,560 Battles from 1479 B.C. to the Present, David Eggenberger. Essential details of every major battle in recorded history from the first battle of Megiddo in 1479 B.C. to Grenada in 1984. List of Battle Maps. New Appendix covering the years 1967-1984. Index. 99 illustrations. 544pp. 6½ x 9¼. 24913-1

SAILING ALONE AROUND THE WORLD, Captain Joshua Slocum. First man to sail around the world, alone, in small boat. One of great feats of seamanship told in delightful manner. 67 illustrations. 294pp. 5⅜ x 8½. 20326-3

ANARCHISM AND OTHER ESSAYS, Emma Goldman. Powerful, penetrating, prophetic essays on direct action, role of minorities, prison reform, puritan hypocrisy, violence, etc. 271pp. 5⅜ x 8½. 22484-8

MYTHS OF THE HINDUS AND BUDDHISTS, Ananda K. Coomaraswamy and Sister Nivedita. Great stories of the epics; deeds of Krishna, Shiva, taken from puranas, Vedas, folk tales; etc. 32 illustrations. 400pp. 5⅜ x 8½. 21759-0

THE TRAUMA OF BIRTH, Otto Rank. Rank's controversial thesis that anxiety neurosis is caused by profound psychological trauma which occurs at birth. 256pp. 5⅜ x 8½. 27974-X

A THEOLOGICO-POLITICAL TREATISE, Benedict Spinoza. Also contains unfinished Political Treatise. Great classic on religious liberty, theory of government on common consent. R. Elwes translation. Total of 421pp. 5⅜ x 8½. 20249-6

THE WIT AND HUMOR OF OSCAR WILDE, Alvin Redman (ed.). More than 1,000 ripostes, paradoxes, wisecracks: Work is the curse of the drinking classes; I can resist everything except temptation; etc. 258pp. 5⅜ x 8½. 20602-5

SHAKESPEARE LEXICON AND QUOTATION DICTIONARY, Alexander Schmidt. Full definitions, locations, shades of meaning in every word in plays and poems. More than 50,000 exact quotations. 1,485pp. 6½ x 9¼. 2-vol. set.
Vol. 1: 22726-X
Vol. 2: 22727-8

SELECTED POEMS, Emily Dickinson. Over 100 best-known, best-loved poems by one of America's foremost poets, reprinted from authoritative early editions. No comparable edition at this price. Index of first lines. 64pp. 5³⁄₁₆ x 8¼. 26466-1

THE INSIDIOUS DR. FU-MANCHU, Sax Rohmer. The first of the popular mystery series introduces a pair of English detectives to their archnemesis, the diabolical Dr. Fu-Manchu. Flavorful atmosphere, fast-paced action, and colorful characters enliven this classic of the genre. 208pp. 5³⁄₁₆ x 8¼. 29898-1

THE MALLEUS MALEFICARUM OF KRAMER AND SPRENGER, translated by Montague Summers. Full text of most important witchhunter's "bible," used by both Catholics and Protestants. 278pp. 6⅝ x 10. 22802-9

SPANISH STORIES/CUENTOS ESPAÑOLES: A Dual-Language Book, Angel Flores (ed.). Unique format offers 13 great stories in Spanish by Cervantes, Borges, others. Faithful English translations on facing pages. 352pp. 5⅜ x 8½. 25399-6

GARDEN CITY, LONG ISLAND, IN EARLY PHOTOGRAPHS, 1869–1919, Mildred H. Smith. Handsome treasury of 118 vintage pictures, accompanied by carefully researched captions, document the Garden City Hotel fire (1899), the Vanderbilt Cup Race (1908), the first airmail flight departing from the Nassau Boulevard Aerodrome (1911), and much more. 96pp. 8⅞ x 11¾. 40669-5

OLD QUEENS, N.Y., IN EARLY PHOTOGRAPHS, Vincent F. Seyfried and William Asadorian. Over 160 rare photographs of Maspeth, Jamaica, Jackson Heights, and other areas. Vintage views of DeWitt Clinton mansion, 1939 World's Fair and more. Captions. 192pp. 8⅞ x 11. 26358-4

CAPTURED BY THE INDIANS: 15 Firsthand Accounts, 1750-1870, Frederick Drimmer. Astounding true historical accounts of grisly torture, bloody conflicts, relentless pursuits, miraculous escapes and more, by people who lived to tell the tale. 384pp. 5⅜ x 8½. 24901-8

THE WORLD'S GREAT SPEECHES (Fourth Enlarged Edition), Lewis Copeland, Lawrence W. Lamm, and Stephen J. McKenna. Nearly 300 speeches provide public speakers with a wealth of updated quotes and inspiration—from Pericles' funeral oration and William Jennings Bryan's "Cross of Gold Speech" to Malcolm X's powerful words on the Black Revolution and Earl of Spenser's tribute to his sister, Diana, Princess of Wales. 944pp. 5⅜ x 8⅜. 40903-1

THE BOOK OF THE SWORD, Sir Richard F. Burton. Great Victorian scholar/adventurer's eloquent, erudite history of the "queen of weapons"—from prehistory to early Roman Empire. Evolution and development of early swords, variations (sabre, broadsword, cutlass, scimitar, etc.), much more. 336pp. 6⅛ x 9¼. 25434-8

CATALOG OF DOVER BOOKS

AUTOBIOGRAPHY: The Story of My Experiments with Truth, Mohandas K. Gandhi. Boyhood, legal studies, purification, the growth of the Satyagraha (nonviolent protest) movement. Critical, inspiring work of the man responsible for the freedom of India. 480pp. 5⅜ x 8½. (Available in U.S. only.) 24593-4

CELTIC MYTHS AND LEGENDS, T. W. Rolleston. Masterful retelling of Irish and Welsh stories and tales. Cuchulain, King Arthur, Deirdre, the Grail, many more. First paperback edition. 58 full-page illustrations. 512pp. 5⅜ x 8½. 26507-2

THE PRINCIPLES OF PSYCHOLOGY, William James. Famous long course complete, unabridged. Stream of thought, time perception, memory, experimental methods; great work decades ahead of its time. 94 figures. 1,391pp. 5⅜ x 8½. 2-vol. set.
Vol. I: 20381-6 Vol. II: 20382-4

THE WORLD AS WILL AND REPRESENTATION, Arthur Schopenhauer. Definitive English translation of Schopenhauer's life work, correcting more than 1,000 errors, omissions in earlier translations. Translated by E. F. J. Payne. Total of 1,269pp. 5⅜ x 8½. 2-vol. set. Vol. 1: 21761-2 Vol. 2: 21762-0

MAGIC AND MYSTERY IN TIBET, Madame Alexandra David-Neel. Experiences among lamas, magicians, sages, sorcerers, Bonpa wizards. A true psychic discovery. 32 illustrations. 321pp. 5⅜ x 8½. (Available in U.S. only.) 22682-4

THE EGYPTIAN BOOK OF THE DEAD, E. A. Wallis Budge. Complete reproduction of Ani's papyrus, finest ever found. Full hieroglyphic text, interlinear transliteration, word-for-word translation, smooth translation. 533pp. 6½ x 9¼. 21866-X

MATHEMATICS FOR THE NONMATHEMATICIAN, Morris Kline. Detailed, college-level treatment of mathematics in cultural and historical context, with numerous exercises. Recommended Reading Lists. Tables. Numerous figures. 641pp. 5⅜ x 8½. 24823-2

PROBABILISTIC METHODS IN THE THEORY OF STRUCTURES, Isaac Elishakoff. Well-written introduction covers the elements of the theory of probability from two or more random variables, the reliability of such multivariable structures, the theory of random function, Monte Carlo methods of treating problems incapable of exact solution, and more. Examples. 502pp. 5⅜ x 8½. 40691-1

THE RIME OF THE ANCIENT MARINER, Gustave Doré, S. T. Coleridge. Doré's finest work; 34 plates capture moods, subtleties of poem. Flawless full-size reproductions printed on facing pages with authoritative text of poem. "Beautiful. Simply beautiful."–*Publisher's Weekly.* 77pp. 9¼ x 12. 22305-1

NORTH AMERICAN INDIAN DESIGNS FOR ARTISTS AND CRAFTSPEOPLE, Eva Wilson. Over 360 authentic copyright-free designs adapted from Navajo blankets, Hopi pottery, Sioux buffalo hides, more. Geometrics, symbolic figures, plant and animal motifs, etc. 128pp. 8⅜ x 11. (Not for sale in the United Kingdom.) 25341-4

SCULPTURE: Principles and Practice, Louis Slobodkin. Step-by-step approach to clay, plaster, metals, stone; classical and modern. 253 drawings, photos. 255pp. 8⅛ x 11. 22960-2

THE INFLUENCE OF SEA POWER UPON HISTORY, 1660–1783, A. T. Mahan. Influential classic of naval history and tactics still used as text in war colleges. First paperback edition. 4 maps. 24 battle plans. 640pp. 5⅜ x 8½. 25509-3

CATALOG OF DOVER BOOKS

THE STORY OF THE TITANIC AS TOLD BY ITS SURVIVORS, Jack Winocour (ed.). What it was really like. Panic, despair, shocking inefficiency, and a little heroism. More thrilling than any fictional account. 26 illustrations. 320pp. 5⅜ x 8½. 20610-6

FAIRY AND FOLK TALES OF THE IRISH PEASANTRY, William Butler Yeats (ed.). Treasury of 64 tales from the twilight world of Celtic myth and legend: "The Soul Cages," "The Kildare Pooka," "King O'Toole and his Goose," many more. Introduction and Notes by W. B. Yeats. 352pp. 5⅜ x 8½. 26941-8

BUDDHIST MAHAYANA TEXTS, E. B. Cowell and others (eds.). Superb, accurate translations of basic documents in Mahayana Buddhism, highly important in history of religions. The Buddha-karita of Asvaghosha, Larger Sukhavativyuha, more. 448pp. 5⅜ x 8½. 25552-2

ONE TWO THREE . . . INFINITY: Facts and Speculations of Science, George Gamow. Great physicist's fascinating, readable overview of contemporary science: number theory, relativity, fourth dimension, entropy, genes, atomic structure, much more. 128 illustrations. Index. 352pp. 5⅜ x 8½. 25664-2

EXPERIMENTATION AND MEASUREMENT, W. J. Youden. Introductory manual explains laws of measurement in simple terms and offers tips for achieving accuracy and minimizing errors. Mathematics of measurement, use of instruments, experimenting with machines. 1994 edition. Foreword. Preface. Introduction. Epilogue. Selected Readings. Glossary. Index. Tables and figures. 128pp. 5⅜ x 8½. 40451-X

DALÍ ON MODERN ART: The Cuckolds of Antiquated Modern Art, Salvador Dalí. Influential painter skewers modern art and its practitioners. Outrageous evaluations of Picasso, Cézanne, Turner, more. 15 renderings of paintings discussed. 44 calligraphic decorations by Dalí. 96pp. 5⅜ x 8½. (Available in U.S. only.) 29220-7

ANTIQUE PLAYING CARDS: A Pictorial History, Henry René D'Allemagne. Over 900 elaborate, decorative images from rare playing cards (14th–20th centuries): Bacchus, death, dancing dogs, hunting scenes, royal coats of arms, players cheating, much more. 96pp. 9¼ x 12¼. 29265-7

MAKING FURNITURE MASTERPIECES: 30 Projects with Measured Drawings, Franklin H. Gottshall. Step-by-step instructions, illustrations for constructing handsome, useful pieces, among them a Sheraton desk, Chippendale chair, Spanish desk, Queen Anne table and a William and Mary dressing mirror. 224pp. 8⅛ x 11¼. 29338-6

THE FOSSIL BOOK: A Record of Prehistoric Life, Patricia V. Rich et al. Profusely illustrated definitive guide covers everything from single-celled organisms and dinosaurs to birds and mammals and the interplay between climate and man. Over 1,500 illustrations. 760pp. 7½ x 10⅛. 29371-8

Paperbound unless otherwise indicated. Available at your book dealer, online at **www.doverpublications.com**, or by writing to Dept. GI, Dover Publications, Inc., 31 East 2nd Street, Mineola, NY 11501. For current price information or for free catalogues (please indicate field of interest), write to Dover Publications or log on to **www.doverpublications.com** and see every Dover book in print. Dover publishes more than 500 books each year on science, elementary and advanced mathematics, biology, music, art, literary history, social sciences, and other areas.